PARTICK CURLING CLUB 1842-1970

Partick Curling Club
1842 - 1970

BY

J. DUNCAN CRAN

PRINTED BY
WILLIAM HODGE AND COMPANY LIMITED
GLASGOW

NOTE

THE author of this history was, at the time of his death, Honorary President of Partick Curling Club. It is not given to many men to be curling at the ripe old age of eighty-eight but such was his good fortune. In addition to the respect which old age begets, he inspired an unusually warm affection in people, some of whom were only half his age, and was a great favourite in the circles in which he moved.

Born in Leith, he married a Partick lady and came to Glasgow during the slump following the first World War. He shared his curling loyalties between Partick and the Watsonian Club and was held in equal esteem by both clubs. Not unnaturally these qualities led to his being elected to office in various curling circles and he was President of Tenth (Dunbartonshire) Province and a Member of the Council of the Royal Caledonian Curling Club.

To the writing of this history he devoted a great deal of time and diligence and it served to fill the gap when he lost his wife and they had no family to help heal the wound. He delved into official curling histories, old newspaper files and club and other Minute Books with meticulous care and the result is contained in the following pages. One hopes it will provide much of interest to the reader and tell the story of a club, based primarily on a locality, which has thrived for over a hundred years and provided us with all that is best in the game which we all enjoy.

DAVID W. ROBINSON
Vice-President,
June, 1971   Royal Caledonian Curling Club.

PREFACE

At an Annual General Meeting of the Partick Curling Club about two years ago a member who had been intelligently browsing through the Minute books said he found them so interesting that he considered them worthy of editing with a view to being reproduced in book form, for circulation among the members and friends. The meeting adopted the suggestion, discussed whom they should approach to undertake this work, and appointed a deputation to call upon me. They argued that firstly I personally had known more of the Office-Bearers and Members before the 1914-18 war than any other member now on the roll, and secondly as I recently retired from business I had nothing better to do! While it was impossible to escape from the truth of these statements, I agreed to do the best I could for the club, whose members had given me so much pleasure in playing the game during the previous forty years, not to mention the consequent companionship and well-being achieved with its opponents.

With errors and omissions, of which there may be many, excepted, here is the result of my efforts to give effect to the commission entrusted to me, aided by such research into the progress of the game during the 121 years since the club was affiliated to the R.C.C.C.

J. Duncan Cran

INTRODUCTION

UNTIL the beginning of the nineteenth century it would seem that games of Curling, although played in many parts of Scotland south of the Grampians and probably mainly in the south-west—Dunbartonshire to the Solway Firth—were more or less confined to the Parishes; and that matches and bonspiels were arranged with neighbouring towns or communities. During the latter half of the eighteenth century roads had been greatly improved and communications between places further apart were becoming easier. Railways did not yet exist, but the Royal Caledonian Curling Club Annual of 1847 contains an article (pp. 147-150) on 'Prospective Advantages of Railways to Curlers'. That article concludes 'We have made these remarks, because we have no doubt that as our railway system becomes extended, the uncertainties alluded to will be very greatly modified and the ease and quickness with which curlers and their stones may be transported to and from suitable fields of ice will be immensely increased . . . we should like therefore, that the Royal Club were to consider the propriety of sheets of shallow water being procured in juxtaposition with some one or more of our leading lines of railway . . . one reason for preferring the "Caledonian" as a main line to any other is that its patronymic is already ours, and that they would certainly lose nothing in showing their goodwill to one of the ancient games of Caledonia, by helping on a general rendezvous in curling weather for the R.C.C.C.'

The French Revolution in the last decade of the eighteenth century followed by the Napoleonic wars on the Continent, in which this country greatly was involved must have occupied and affected the minds and activities of the people. These extraneous disturbances however do not seem to have perturbed those Scots curlers, who, when Jack Frost obliged, laid down their implements and tools and found their ways to the frozen waters; or even to have upset the golfers, particularly in the Lothians and Fifeshire, who continued to spend their leisure hours driving their feathered cored balls over the links.

It is quite remarkable how many Curling Clubs and Societies were instituted during the first forty years after 1800, and how also quite a number of Golf Clubs were founded during that period. The Revd. John Kerr's *History of Curling*, published 1890 (pp. 172-175), gives the number of Curling Societies and Clubs known to have been instituted between 1800 and 1838, when the Royal Club was founded, as 133. We therefore may assume that men felt that these above-mentioned disturbances were of the past and that the social side of life should now be encouraged. In what better way than by forming societies and clubs for the improvement of their pastimes and the consolidation of the constitutions and rules governing their respective games, as had already been done by the earlier clubs instituted in the previous century.

It is interesting to note that four publications appeared during this period from 1800 to the foundation of the Royal Club in 1838. The first was the *Account of the Game of Curling* by a member of the Duddingston Curling Society (Revd. James Ramsay, later minister of Gladsmuir, East Lothian), published 1811. It gives a very good description of the game and how it is played, includes relative quotations from the Scottish poets—Pennycuick, Graeme and Davidson, and concludes with the Rules of Curling to be observed by Duddingston Curling Society and the remark 'The above rules received the approbation and sanction of a general meeting of the society held in the Curlers' Hall, Duddingston, upon the 6th January, 1804'. The *Channel Stane*, Fourth Series, 1884, says 'Ramsay's Account of the Game of Curling is the first history of the Game'.

The *Kilmarnock Treatise on Curling* was first published in 1828, and privately reprinted in Edinburgh in 1883 (250 copies). The 1828 publication is entitled 'A Descriptive and Historical Sketch of Curling; also Rules Practical directions, songs, toasts, and a Glossary' . . . It is remarkable that, while it gives poems and songs by Sir Alexander Boswell, 'The Ettrick Shepherd,' and other lesser known poets, it has no quotation from Burns, whose poems were first published in Kilmarnock, 1786.

Then we have *Memorabilia Curliana Mabenensia* by Sir Richard Brown, published Dumfries, 1830. The frontispiece has two small engravings of Lochmaben and Duddingston Loch and four figures in the attitude of delivering curling stones. The author, in his preliminary chapter says—'It is a game where all parties and persons amalgamate; and where that reciprocity of cordiality and good feeling prevails by which the fellowship of the olden day is cherished and kept alive in the present piping times of politics and peace'. We may assume that they then were feeling much as we do today in this A.D. 1970. We also have our politics and peace, though some may not describe the period as 'piping times'. The author also made the following characteristic observations about the game—'It rouses the social warmth which the howling winds of winter have torpified; kicks out of the penthouse of the mind the chimeras engendered by the leisure perusal of the Dumfries Journals, and lastly, begets in the gastronomical region one of those important vacuums, into which are cast those gaseous vapours that cloud and distemper the brain, and which when buried under a trebly replenished plate of beef and greens, with a quantum suff. of whisky toddy, would require even a more startling apparition than the ghost of the Catholic Question, a personification of the National Debt, or any other political bugbear of the day, to arise from the abyss wherein they have fallen, and extricate them from that load under which they are quickly inurned' . . . 'written like a true curler commented 'Christopher North' in his article 'Curliana' in *Blackwood's Magazine*, December, 1831. This book includes descriptions of historical reference to curlers, of how the game is played, and of the stones used, of artificial rinks, and of the bonspiels between the Lochmaben and Closeburn Clubs. Then follow many songs and poems, rules on curling, toasts and sayings, and a glossary of terms and phrases used by curlers.

Curling and Artificial Pond Making by Dr. John Cairnie of Largs was published in Glasgow, 1833. This book devotes much space to the Artificial Pond and includes Rules for Curling at Largs, the sizes and weights of stones, and particulars of crampits, brooms, and other details. Among many clubs in the south-west of Scotland he mentions are several in the neighbourhood of Glasgow . . . 'there has been a curling club upwards of sixty years in the Burgh of Anderston under the direction of A Preses, Treasurer, and seven Managers. There are also clubs in the following places . . . North Woodside, Gorbals, Partick, Govan, Pollokshaws, Cathcart, and Port Dundas, all under a regular board of directors,' poems and songs, a list of curling phrases and toasts, and a plan for artificial rinks are included.

In the magazine world of this period Blackwood's, first published in April 1817 and 'still going strong,' contained several articles on winter sports; the first of which in February 1820, entitled Horae Scoticae No. 1 gave a caricaturing account of a bonspiel between Lochmaben and Closeburn curling clubs by 'Peter MacFinn' (The Revd. Professor Gillespie), Helmorran Manse. Thereafter for some years occasional articles appeared from the pens of 'Christopher North' and others till in 1831 an article 'Curliana' dealt with and criticised Sir Richard Brown's *Memorabilia Curliana Mabenensia,* and quoted from it this paragraph . . . 'Fishing is indeed a most bewitching amusement, and it would be something approaching sacrilege in me to under-rate its claims . . . but curling is, undoubtedly, the more manly, and by far the more social of the two. In the former case, one must be alone to enjoy the sport in perfection . . . In the case of curling, man is leagued with and opposed to man. It is most essentially social, and whilst it calls into action strength and muscular exertion . . . whilst it presupposes skill and address, it invigorates the body and braces the mind. What has been beautifully, because justly said of a more serious predicament, is exhibited literally on the rink—"There the rich and the poor meet together, and the servant is free from his master. This is indeed the Saturnalia of Scotland".'

And the above-mentioned *Kilmarnock Treatise* includes among its songs one published by Blackwood—'In spring what lovely days' (air—'Thou has left me ever Jamie')—the last verse of which is:

> 'Let others haunt the festive-hall,
> Where wine-cups sparkle bright,
> The witchery of the crowded ball,
> Illumed by beauty's light;
> But give to me the frozen lake,
> All crowded to the brink,
> Where joyful shouts of victory break
> From every ardent rink.'

As a result of the increased interest in the game throughout the country, and of the above-mentioned publications and articles in magazines, and, most important of all, the want of some generally approved code of rules for the conduct of the game, there was published early 1838—'*Laws in Curling*; with notes by Petrostes, printed for J. Whitehead, Kinross, and Maclachlan and Stewart, Edinburgh. 5m quarto, sewed, pp. 25.' The author was Professor George Walker Arnott of the Orwell Club, and his 'Laws' 'are principally founded on those framed by Lochmaben'.[1]

On p. 11 of his pamphlet[2] Arnott referred to the 'many points

[1] Kerr's *History*, p. 214.
[2] Kerr's *History*, p. 232.

left to be settled by curlers before a match began' and made a practical suggestion 'That this might be easily remedied by a convention formed of the secretaries or some accredited office-bearers of the principal initiated clubs of Scotland'.

Some unknown person, following up this suggestion, inserted in the *North British Advertiser* of May 26th 1838 the following advertisement—'To curlers—In consequence of what is suggested at p. 11 of the *Laws in Curling* (a pamphlet just published by Maclauchlan and Stewart, Edinburgh), it is hoped that the initiated curling clubs in Scotland will depute one of the Brethern of their Court to meet in the Waterloo Hotel, Edinburgh on Wednesday, the 20th June next at 11 o'clock, a.m., for the purpose of making the mysteries more uniform in future, and, if possible, to form a Grand Court, to which all provincial ones shall be subject and to elect a Grand President, with other office-bearers. It is hoped that all Brethern, who see this notice will direct the attention of their President or Secretary to it without delay. 16th May 1838'.

The meeting was held, John Cairnie of Curling Hall being made Chairman. No regular minute of their doings was taken but in the *North British Advertiser* and other papers an advertisement drawn up by the company soon thereafter appeared:

'To curlers—In consequence of an advertisement which appeared in the *North British Advertiser* on 26th May 1838 a meeting of curlers was held on the 20th inst., John Cairnie, Esq., of Curling Hall, Largs, in the chair. Deputations from various clubs appeared, who approved generally . . . but, anxious for a fuller representation of clubs throughout the country . . . they adjourned to Wednesday 25th July next at 12 o'clock in the Waterloo Hotel, when they hope the different clubs of Scotland will make a point of sending deputations. sgd. John Cairnie, chairman.' The meeting was held; forty-four gentlemen represented thirty-six clubs. Resolution was passed 'That this meeting do form itself into a club, composed of the different initiated clubs of Scotland, under the name of the Grand Caledonian Curling Club.' Soon thereafter office-bearers were appointed, who framed constitution and rules and produced reports. A year later appeared the first number of the *Annual of the Grand Caledonian Curling Club*, which since then has regularly appeared.

Four years later, the club being well and truly established, in 1842, when Her Majesty the Queen[1] and the Prince Consort visited Scotland, they were entertained by the Earl of Mansfield, then President of the Grand Club at the palace of Scone. The curlers requested Lord Mansfield to present Prince Albert with a pair of curling stones, which the latter graciously accepted, and at once assented to the suggestion that he should be Patron of the Club. Her Majesty made particular inquiries of the Earl regarding the game of curling, and a demonstration was given on the polished oaken floor of the room. In the following year a petition was sent by the Grand Club to Sir George Clerk, for presentation to the Queen, praying Her Majesty to allow the use of the term Royal. The reply was sent through Sir James Graham, Secretary of the Home Department to William Gibson-Craig, Esq., the President of the Club and was as follows—'Whitehall, 12th August 1843—Sir, I am directed by Secretary Sir James Graham to inform you that he has laid before the Queen the petition of the Grand Caledonian Curling Club, praying that they may be permitted to assume the designation of the "Royal Grand Caledonian Curling Club", and I am to acquaint you that Her Majesty has been graciously pleased to grant the prayer of the petition. I have the honour to be, etc. H. Marmers Sutton.'

'The adjective Grand being deemed superfluous, permission was given to drop it, and since that time the Club has worn its present title.'

[1] Kerr's *History*, pp. 242/3.

PARTICK DURING THE 19TH CENTURY

A FEW superficial notes on Partick at the time of the institution of the club and during the next fifty years are of interest.

The village was more or less confined to the triangular area enclosed on the north by Dumbarton Road westwards from the then new bridge over the Kelvin, still to be seen just upstream from the present highway bridge; on the east by the right or west bank of the Kelvin to its junction with the Clyde at Meadowside, where then was the shipyard of Tod and McGregor; and on the west from Meadowside to Dumbarton Road by Cow Lane, later Orchard Street, and now probably Merkland Street. From the Cross on Dumbarton Road, and opposite the foot of Byres Road two roads branched off, as they still do—Old Dumbarton Road or Bridge Street as it was called leading to the then old bridge (since rebuilt) thence to Overnewton and Anderston; and Castlebank Street, then known as Cooperswell Road and lower down as Meadow Road at Meadowside. Castlebank Street had branches off leading to the Kelvin—Knowe Brae, Kilbrae, and Horse Brae (near Merkland Farm). There were also some buildings, including the Church, in and around the triangle formed by Dumbarton Road, Byres Road, and Church Street. Gilmourhill Mansion House stood where the University now is and University Avenue was then known as Woodside Road, and probably remained so till the University moved there, its foundation stone being laid by the Prince of Wales, who with the Princess, visited Glasgow in 1868. There were no buildings on either side of Byres Road north from its junction with Church Street till the one now known as the 'Curlers Tavern'.

Prior to 1830 the inhabitants were employed in the many meal and flour mills, in handloom weaving and in the bleaching and printing works. About 1830 the first shipbuilding yard was established at Meadowside by Tod and McGregor, who launched their first iron ship in 1835. This yard was bought by David and William Henderson in the early eighteen seventies. In 1838 Robinson Dunn & Co. started their Partick Sawmill, only recently transferring their business to Temple, Anniesland, where they also had a sawmill. Thereafter in 1862 A. & J. Inglis established their shipbuilding and engineering works at Pointhouse. Other trades and industries were attracted by these developments and the population rapidly increased from 3,184 in 1841 to 17,693 by 1871.

Thatched cottages were quickly being displaced by slated houses and tenements during these years of rapid extension, and owing to complaints of poor drainage, want of street lighting and inadequate police supervision, the village was constituted in 1852 into a burgh under the management of a Council of twelve members, of these the following office-bearers of Partick Curling Club were elected members of the first Town Council—David Tod of Ironbank, Provost, and John White of Scotstoun Mills, a Councillor. Thus early were members of the club taking a prominent part in local public affairs.

Other sports and games clubs have been particularly identified with the burgh and came into being during the latter half of the century. The West of Scotland Cricket Club was established in Hamilton Crescent in 1862, and, after more than a century, is still going strong in that famous ground. The Partick Thistle Football Club ('The Jaggs'), formed in 1876 from a former Partick F.C., played on several grounds in Partick till in 1912 it moved to its present ground in Firhill. The West of Scotland Rugby Football Club was and is a notable Scottish Rugby Club. It played on the Cricket Club's grounds at Hamilton Crescent till 1939. Since the war it obtained ground and now plays at Burnbrae, Milngavie. There was also a junior rugby club with ground in Partickhill. Tennis and Bowling Clubs thrived, the Partick Tennis Club being one of the leading ones in the west of Scotland, with its courts and clubhouse in Balshagray Avenue, adjoining the present clubhouse and rinks of the Curling Club. The tennis club ceased to function after the last war.

PARTICK CURLING CLUB

THE first volume of minutes is titled 'Partick Union Curling Society Book' and covers the period from its institution April 1842 to January 1881.

Considering the times in which these minutes were written and of which they give a remarkably good record of the meetings and doings of the club, one must admire the good hand-writing throughout the greater part of the volume. The club secretaries whose hands penned them, must have been educated in the old parish schools, had been well grounded in the three R's and could put words together in an intelligent way. With rare exceptions their records are easily read. Sometimes the spelling, even of men's names, is phonetic, but, if one has been living in Clydeside many years, it is not difficult to decipher the meaning. In a few isolated cases one cannot be certain that one's transcription is the correct one.

The first page details the 'Rules of Curling on the Ice'. Thirteen of these more or less follow the twelve given in 'An Account of the Game of Curling' by a member of the Duddingston Curling Society, published Edinburgh 1811. However, on going more closely into the matter of these early recorded rules, we find that those enumerated by the Partick Society are nearly a verbatim copy of those given by Dr. Cairnie in his 'Essay on Curling'. This work includes not only these original Duddingston rules, but an additional seven with penalties for non-observance of the same, which the worthy Doctor evidently found necessary for the curlers in Largs. His use in Rule 12 of the clause 'the players may advise in a whisper' induces a touch of humour into a rule for 'The Roaring Game'.

RULES OF CURLING ON THE ICE

1. A rink is commonly made from 36 to 44 yards inclusive. When a game is begun neither the rinks nor the stones are to be changed or altered unless by the consent of a majority of the players.

2. The Hog score to be one-sixth part of the length of the entire rink and every stone to be deemed a Hog, the sole of which does not completely cover the score.

3. The foot-iron being properly placed, the ice is to be scratched so as it may be constantly laid on the same place—upon the left side of the Tozee. The same thing is to be done, if there be any left-handed players, by a scratch upon the right. The foot-iron may be placed near the Tozee or some distance behind it but in every situation the stone played should pass over it.

4. The order of playing adopted at the beginning should be observed till the end of the game.

5. All stones should be perfectly circular and, unless broken, no stone is to be changed throughout the game, and then the largest portion of the stone shall count. If a stone roll or is upset, it is to be placed upon its bottom wherever it stops.

6. Every stone shall be reckoned as played when the player parts with the handle; but should he fall and retain his hold, although the stone may have parted from the handle, he shall be allowed to play it again.

7. A player may sweep his stone the whole length of the rink. His party not until it has passed the hog-score. The opposite party not to sweep till the stone has passed the Tozee.

8. Should a stone be marred by the party to which it belongs it is to be reckoned a burnt stone and put off the ice; if marred by the adverse party, it should be placed agreeably to the directions given unless it be very evident it was marred from accident, in which case it should be played over again. Should a resting stone be marred accidentally it is to be put as nearly as possible in its former position.

9. Players moving upon the ice should invariably keep to the right in going up or coming down; and this is particularly necessary in artificial ponds when the curb stone is not broad enough to allow two persons meeting to pass.

10. A stone played out of turn should be stopped in its progress or the head may be disputed if the stone rest so as to injure the party whose right it was to play.

11. No measuring allowable till the end of the head, and all disputed shots to be referred to a neutral person.

12. The directors, hin, han's,[1] doupers,[2] or skippers shall have the exclusive regulation of the game and the players may advise in a whisper, but cannot control their directions. Each director may name a vice to take his place when he is about to play, and every player to follow the directions given.

13. Every player to be ready when his time comes and to take only a reasonable time to play. If by mistake he plays a wrong stone it must be replaced by the one he intended to play.

14. Left-handed players are bound to replace the foot-iron on the right side of the Tozee under a penalty of one gill of whisky every time they neglect to do so.

15. Any player placing the foot-iron out of the line of the scratch shall forfeit his shot.

16. No player to cross or go on the middle of the rink.

17. A player with a double-bottomed stone shall not be allowed to turn it during the game.

18. Players coming without a broom are liable to a fine.

19. Unfair footing forfeits the shot.

20. No piked crampets to be allowed on the ice on any account.

[1] Hin 'han' (or Hin 'Haun')—'The person who plays last in order in his party'—*The Kilmarnock Treatise*, p. 79.

[2] Douper—skip—with footnote 'The designation "skipper" or "skip" is not found in the last century (i.e., 18th) records examined by us'—Kerr's *History*, pp. 157/8.

1842-1860

THE next few pages contain the list of members of the Society, with the years of their admission from 1842 to 1849 when the Partick Curling Club, as it had become designated, was admitted to the Royal Caledonian Curling Club. Thereafter this list in the Minute Book was not added to or kept up-to-date. We must assume that the later secretaries had their own ways of keeping the roll of members, since they annually had to submit to the Secretary of the Royal Club a list of the names of regular and occasional members. After 1939 however only the number of regular members had to be submitted.

On the following pages of this Minute Book the minutes of general and committee meetings and other incidental information are recorded.

The Society was started by a group of Partick Curlers. They previously must have played their games and presumably matches with such neighbouring societies or clubs as Govan (instituted 1725), Anderston (1773),[1] Yoker (1796),[1] Kelvindock (1813),[1] North Woodside (1819), and Willowbank (1837). They met in the house of John Adams, spirit merchant, Burns Cottage, Partick, with the object of forming a society, and there and then appointed office-bearers to carry out their decisions. The minute of that meeting reads:

'The first general meeting of the Partick Union Curling Society was held on Friday the first day of April eighteen hundred and forty-two in Burns Cottage, Partick, when the following persons were nominated as office-bearers and directors of the said Society:

    Mr. John McMaster   — *President*
    Mr. John Seton   — *Treasurer*
    Mr. James Borthwick — *Secretary*

Members of committee nominated for 1842:

    Mr. Adam Craig
    Mr. John Anderson
    Mr. William Anderson
    Mr. Alexander Baird.'

The next minute is of 'a meeting of the committee—held in the house of Thomas Craig, carter, Partick on the 24th November for

[1] Kerr's *History*, p. 115.

the purpose of entering new members, etc., etc. It was also agreed to by the committee that a meeting should be held in Burns Cottage on the second Friday of December for the purpose of electing the Board of Directors, receiving payments, entering new members, etc., etc.'

Then follows the minute of 'a general meeting of the Society was held in Burns Cottage on the 9th of December. The old Board of Directors was re-elected, members of committee re-elected, etc., for 1843. A committee was elected for the management of the dinner on Christmas Eve—William Anderson, Adam Craig, John McMaster and John Seton. The following members were Regularly Brothered to the Society William McIndoe, Hugh Miller, John Adam and John White. Alexander Baird the Grand Master of the said Society, John McMaster, James Brothwick, John Seton, John Anderson, William Anderson, Adam Craig, and John Wilson was renewed in their Brothership.'

'The annual meeting of the Society took place in the House of Mr. Sinclair, grocer and spirit dealer, Partick, on Monday the 25th December 1842 when 14 members[1] of said Society sat down to an excellent dinner provided by said Mr. Sinclair. Each man paid 1/6d. for dinner.[2] The chair was filled by Alexr. Baird, printer. John Seton acted as croupier. After the usual toasts was given from the chair the healths of the several office bearers of the Society was drunk and responded to. The songs and chat was kept up with great glee till an early hour in the morning when all parted in good friendship. There was three new members and six brothers to the Society, namely Peter Barr, James Bennie, John Sinclair, Thomas Craig, Robert Barr, James Weir. The above six members brothered to the Society.'

It seems to have been a successful first annual meeting.

'A general meeting of the Society took place in the House of John Adams, Burns Cottage, Partick on the 12th December 1843, when John Anderson was elected President, John Seton Treasurer, and James Brothwick Secretary to said Society. Members of committee nominated for 1843, namely William Anderson, John McLaren, John McMaster, Alexander Baird, James Bennie nomin-

[1] According to the list of members on the pages before the minutes start there were 17 elected during 1842.
[2] Kerr's *History*, p. 218.

ated as officer for the current year. James Smith and John Harvie, new members, both Brothered to Society. A committee was elected for the management of a dinner on Christmas Eve, namely Adam Craig, William Anderson, John Anderson, John McMaster.'

'The annual meeting of the Society took place in the House of James Wear, spirit dealer, Partick on the evening of the 25th December 1843, when 14 members of said Society sat down to an excellent dinner provided by said James Wear. Each man paid 1/6d. for dinner. The chair was filled by John McMaster, late president of the Society. Alexander Baird acted as Croupier. After the usual toasts was given from the chair, the healths of Society and office-bearers was given and responded to. The song and chat was kept up to an early hour next morning, when, at the close of the meeting, it was understood that on the earliest opportunity that John McMaster and John Anderson should play a game at ice for 2/6d. The following was chosen by them at said meeting—

John Anderson's men	John McMaster's men
Alexander Baird	James Borthwick
James Bennie	John Harvie
James Weir	John Adam
James Smith	John McLaren
Adam Craig	John Sinclair
John Wilson	John Smith

The following was nominated as heads of Racks—in Society, John McMaster, John Anderson, James Smith, John Seton.'

Nevertheless 'a meeting of the Society was held in Burns Cottage on 12th January 1844, when it was agreed upon that the heads of racks should choose five players each to play for that season. The following is the result of that meeting—John Anderson, John Seton, John Harvie (in place of James Smith) and James Bennie (in place of John McMaster)' and the names of five members to each, 'according to a former agreement the above named racks played a game on Monday 5th day of February 1844. John McMaster's rack, against John Anderson's rack—the latter came off victorious by six shots; John Seton rack played against James Smith rack, the former came off victorious by twelve shots. Game commenced at 10 o'clock and played till 4 p.m.'[1]

[1] 'Jack Frost' evidently was not much in evidence at that time, as this is the first and only record of a Society game so far.

A committee meeting was held in Burns Cottage on 14th December 1844 when two new members John Roughhead and William Brown—were admitted; and a committee was elected for the management of dinner on Christmas Eve, namely William Anderson, Adam Craig, and James Bennie.

'A general meeting of the Society was held in Mr. John Sinclair's House on the 25th December 1844, when Mr. John Anderson was elected preses, Mr. John Seton Treasurer, and John Smellie Secretary, and Adam Craig, William Anderson, Alexander Baird, and John McMaster members of committee and Thomas Craig Officer. It was agreed at said meeting that there should be no annual dinner as formerly, and that the Society apply to be admitted to the Royal Grand Caledonian Club.' This was not accomplished till 1849.

The decision 'that there should be no annual dinner as formerly' seems a sudden *volte-face*, since only eleven days previous a committee was appointed for the purpose, and minutes of previous annual dinners indicated that these functions had been very successful. Incidentally it is not perhaps an intrusion to remark that in these so-called bad old days there was an advertisement in the *Herald* of 23rd December 1842 as follows—

WHISKY

Great reduction in the price of whisky

Fine Pure Malt Aqua

Warranted Full Strength 110 p. same as from Distillery
at 7/2d. per gallon

Robert Park & Co., wholesale and retail wine and spirit merchants, No. 76 Gallowgate (opposite Nile Street) respectfully beg to acquaint the Trade and the Public in general that they are now selling, for cash, Fine Pure Malt Whisky, warranted full strength, 110 p. same as from distillery. Purchasers of five gallons and upwards allowed a liberal discount on the above.

'A general meeting of the Society was held on 24th December 1845 in Mr. Sinclair's House when Mr. William Anderson was elected Preses, John Seton Treasurer, and John Smellie Secretary; and Robert Calder, John McLaren, John Anderson and James Borthwick members of Committee; and John Sinclair officer. John Calder was brothered to Society and James Smith resigned. John Harvie was made Director in place of James Smith. William

Brown put in place of John Harvie. Peter Barr failing to appear or pay up arrears was put out and John Roughhead was put on John Anderson's rack in his place. Archibald Weir not appearing James Campbell was put on John McMaster's rack in his place.'

The minuting of such details shows there was a strict observance of the rules.

'On the 23rd of December 1846 the Club challenged Govan Club to play sixteen players on Friday the 25th, which was accepted and played at Govan, when the Govan Club came off victorious by twenty-six shots.' No other information is given of this first match with a neighbouring club. We may assume that four rinks a side took part and that these were formed on the lines of those mentioned in the following minute.

'The annual meeting of the Society was held in Mr. John Sinclair's House on the 25th December 1846, when Mr. William Anderson was re-elected Preses, Mr. John Seton re-elected Treasurer, and Mr. John Smellie re-elected Secretary. Mr. John Anderson, John Harvie, James Bennie and James Borthwick members of Committee and John Sinclair officer. Messrs. James Brownlie, Duncan Smith and Alexr. Smellie brothered to Society. Messrs. James Borthwick, James Bennie, and John Smellie were appointed committee to uplift one shilling from each member and join Royal Grand Caledonian Club. It was also agreed that Mr. James Bennie be douper in place of Mr. John McMaster.

Rinks arranged as follows:

John Harvie's	John Anderson's
William McIndoe	James Borthwick
John Smellie	Alexr. Baird
Robert Calder	John Roughead
John Sinclair	Adam Craig
William Brown	Thomas Craig

John Seton's	James Bennie's
Robert Baird	John Wilson
Wm. Anderson	James Weir
John McLaren	Lachlan McKinnon
Hugh Miller	John Adam
John Smith	James Campbell'

PARTICK, 12*th June* 1848

'A deputation of the Partick Curling Club by request of said Club called on James Gibson, Esq., Hillhead to make arrangements regarding that piece of ground for a curling pond situated near the branch of the Western Road leading to Partick, bounded on the North by the property of Matthew Montgomery, Esq., on the south by the property of Dr. Fleming, Partick, and known by the name of Clayholes, and containing about an acre thereby. The said deputation in name of the said Club arranged with the said James Gibson, Esq., to rent the said piece of ground for said purpose for five years from May last at the rent of £2 per annum with the usual conditions connected with ground eligible for feuing. The following are the names of the deputation—William Anderson, Preses; James Borthwick, Secretary; James Smith, Manager.'

CLAYHOLES, 15*th June* 1848

'At a meeting called by the Preses of the Partick Curling Club it was agreed the ground related by the said Club from James Gibson, Esq., should be levelled and put in a proper condition for a curling pond. They accordingly agreed with Thomas Forrest to put in proper order the said pond, that is to level the banks and several small mounds on the ground to the level of the water at that time standing in the low places, and to put earth into the lowest place, in order to make the whole as level as possible.'

'Copy of Lease entered into between the Managers of the Partick Curling Club and James Gibson of Hillhead.

HILLHEAD, 3*rd August* 1848

Messrs. William Anderson, Preses
    ,,   James Bennie, Treasurer
    ,,   James Borthwick, Secretary
to Partick Curling Club
    Gentlemen,

I Hereby agree to give you a lease of five years from Whitsunday last, of a piece of ground part of the lands of Hillhead, for the purpose of being used by the Partick Curling Club as a curling pond.

The piece of ground hereby agreed to be let, is bounded on the North by the centre line of a street called Great George Street on the West partly by the Partick branch of the Great Western Road, partly by the lands of Kelvinside, and partly by the feu belonging to Mr. James Carrick, on the East by the centre line of a street eleven feet west from the wall enclosing the lands belonging to the heirs of the late Robt. Allan, Esq., and on the South by a hedge separating said ground from other parts of the lands of Hillhead.

The yearly rent of said piece of ground hereby agreed to be let is to be two pounds stg. payable half yearly, the first half yearly payment to be at Martinmas first.

Although the lease is to be for five years, yet I reserve power to take the said ground at any time during the said lease if I require it for the purpose of selling or feuing, and if so, it is to be given up by you without any damages or compensation whatever.

> I am, Your most ob. St.,
>
> sgd. JAMES GIBSON.'

On the same date the same three representatives of the Club signed an acceptance of the above offer and agreed to all the conditions thereof.

'The annual meeting of Partick Curling Club was held in Mr. William McIndoe's house on Friday the 9th of December 1848 when the following members was elected as office bearers of said Club—William Anderson as Preses, John Anderson, Treasurer, James Bennie, Vice Preses, and James Borthwick, Secretary. James Brownlie, James Bennie, Alexr. Baird, Peter McGaw, members of the committee. The racks was arranged as follows—John Anderson, John Harvie, James Bennie, John Roughead. It was also agreed at said meeting that printed forms of cards should be got for the use of said club, and that steps should be taken to join the Royal Caledonian Club in Edinburgh. Mr. Roughead and Mr. Morrison was appointed to take charge of this matter at its proper time. It was also agreed that five shillings should be paid by every member joining the Club after this date.'

'At a general meeting of the Partick Curling Club held in Mrs. Sinclair's Curlers' Tavern[1] on 13th March 1849 the following

[1] This is the first mention of a meeting in 'The Curlers' Tavern' which ever since has been known by that euphonious title. We may assume that, since it adjoined the pond then leased from Mr. James Gibson, it easily acquired this significant appellation by the local inhabitants. From early pictures of it, the present building seems little changed in outward appearance from the original one. In the map of 1842, it was the only building on Byres Road (then referred to as Road from Partick) North of the junction of it with Church Street. Meetings in the Club were held in the Tavern at intervals till 1855. The Club in 1856 were obliged to find new ground for their pond and moved West to Peel Street.

members[1] was Initiated into the Royal Caledonian Club and received their diploma attested by the Secretary of the Royal Caledonian Curling Club:

William Anderson, James Borthwick, John Anderson, James Bennie, John Adam, Alexr. Baird, John Harvie, William Brown, James Campbell, John Roughead, Peter McGaw, Andrew Jackson, Adam McAulay, John Morrison, Matthew King, John McKechnie, John White, Hugh Kennedy, Thomas Craig, John McMaster, Hugh Miller, John Fletcher, David Haddow, James Brownlie, Robert Craig.'

'The annual meeting of the Partick Curling Club was held in 1849, Mrs. Sinclair's Curlers Tavern on Thursday the eighth of November when it was proposed by Mr. Morrison and carried unanimously that the whole of the office-bearers for last year should still be kept in office for this year. It was agreed also that 2/6d. be the subscription for the present year from the members.'

In the R.C.C.C. Annual of 1849-50 it is stated that Partick was one of ten clubs admitted.   The entry is as follows:

No. 148—Partick Club
County of Lanark.   Post Town—Partick
Instituted 1842.   Admitted into the Royal Club 1849
James Gibson, Esq., Hillhead, Patron
William Anderson, President
James Bennie, Vice President
John Morrison and John Rochead, Representative members
John Anderson, Treasurer; James Borthwick, Secretary

Committee or Council of management—James Bennie, Adam McAulay, Peter McGaw, James Brownlie, Alexander Baird.
Regular members—30 in number.[2]

[1] This was the first list of initiates into the R.C.C.C.
[2] List from R.C. Annual 1850, p. 161:
William Anderson, John Adam, James Borthwick, John McMaster, James Bennie, John Harvie, John Smith, James Campbell, Peter McGaw, Andrew Jackson, John Morrison, A. M. K. Miller, John White, John Fletcher, James Black, John Anderson, Alexander Baird, Thomas Craig, Hugh Miller, William McIndoe, John McLaren, William Brown, John Rochead, James Brownlee, Adam McAulay, Mathew King, John McKechnie, Hugh Kennedy, David Haddow, Robert Craig.

'4th January, 1850—at a committee meeting held in the House of William Anderson, Preses, the following persons were proposed to be admitted members of the Partick Curling Club—Messrs. William Chalmers, John McConnell, Charles Stewart, Thomas Baird, and George Smellie.'

'8th January, 1850—The handsome silver rink medal, the property of the Club was played for this day according to the rules of the Club, when, after being keenly contested for by the skips and other members. Mr. John Anderson's rink was declared the victors for the year.'

11th January, 1850—Three rinks of the Club—John Anderson, John Rochead, and John Harvie, went to Lochwinnoch to the Grand Caledonian Curling Match. It was played on Barr Meadow[1] and was between clubs on the North and South sides of the Clyde. 127 rinks a side took part and the North won by a majority of 233 shots. New Monkland had the highest up score for the winners— 37 up. The Partick scores were:

John Rochead 12 shots up v. James Lang, Paisley Union.
John Harvie 15 shots up v. Robert Campbell, Lochwinnoch.
John Anderson 7 shots up v. William Connell, Lochwinnoch.

13th January, 1850—Twelve of the young members of the Club met on their pond at Clayholes the twelve members who played at

[1] Mr. Harvey of Castle Semple refused permission for the bonspiel to be played on Lochwinnoch, so it was held on Barr Meadow on a splendid sheet of ice kindly furnished (by flooding the land) for the occasion by the proprietor, Colonel Macdowall of Garthland. Mr. Harvey was offended by the interest the inhabitants took in the matter and raised an action in the Court of Session not only against them but 'all others' from curling, skating or going on the loch in time of frost. Mr. Harvey lost in the lower court, and appealed to the Supreme Court, which gave him a favourable decision on the ground that no servitude could be acquired over water. Mr. Taylor (The Rev. Dr. Jas. Taylor in his *Curling*, published 1884) adds that 'Lord Fullerton, in giving judgement, expressed his regret that such an action had been brought, but added that the Court had no alternative but to grant the interdict craved. The case is fortunately unique and Mr. Harvey's example is not likely to be followed by any Scottish landlord'.

Lochwinnoch to play a game for beef and greens. The ice was keen but very biassed, and the young members lost by 20 shots. After discussing the beef and greens, the President and members of committee being present, it was proposed and a challenge sent to the Govan Club to play sixteen of their members at Partick Curling Club pond, which was accepted for Wednesday 16th inst. Sixteen members of the Govan Curling Club met the members of the Partick Curling Club as arranged. The ice was keen, play commenced at noon and ended at 4 o'clock, when after a keenly contested game the Govan players gained by 13 shots.

17th September, 1850—General meeting held in the house of Mr. Wm. Brown, spirit dealer, Partick for the purpose of electing office-bearers, forming new rinks, and annual report to the Caledonian Club, etc.:

Elected President   —   John White, Scotstoun Mills.
            Vice-Pres.   —   John Adam, Burns Cottage.
            Secretary   —   James Borthwick, gardener.
            Treasurer   —   John Anderson, tea merchant.
Representative members—John Morison and John Rochead.
Committee—Jas. Bennie, Jas. Brownlie, Alexr. Baird, David Haddow, Jas. Campbell.
Heads of rinks—John Anderson, Jas. Borthwick, Jas. Bennie, John Rochead, John Smith, John McMaster, Alexr. Baird.

A week later (24th Sept.) a meeting was held in the house of Wm. Brown, spirit dealer. The following members were initiated into the Royal Club—Thomas Granger, Archd. Anderson, Andrew Roy, Jas. McIver, Jas. Smith, Thos. Smith, David Haddow, Hugh Smith.

In November a committee meeting considered the fencing of the pond. Jas. Borthwick agreed to get the stones from Gilmourhill and John White consented to cart them free of expense.

26th December, 1850—A general meeting in the house of Wm. Chalmers, Newton Place, considered a letter from the Royal Club asking about number of rinks for a Grand Match in January or February on Lindores Loch. Skips for four rinks were named, but the match did not take place. (This is of interest only because this loch is one of the three now considered by the Council of the Royal

Club as suitable for the Grand Match, the others being Loch
Leven and the Lake of Menteith).

From now on we can imagine the office-bearers were finding
more to take up their attention. The admission of the Club to the
Royal Club brought correspondence to and from the secretary in
Edinburgh, and the Representative Members had to be informed
of and consulted about all such communications. There are however
no records for a year or two at this time of any games or matches
on the ice.

28th October, 1851—A general meeting was held in the Curler's
Tavern (Mrs. Sinclair's) for the purpose of electing office-bearers,
etc., and considering letter from Lochwinnoch. It was agreed the
office-bearers be re-elected, and that the racks remain as formerly.
Considering the letter from Lochwinnoch, members were of opinion
that, as it related to a legal question, they would not involve themselves as a club, but sympathise with them, and might at a future
time give a little to help defray expenses. This evidently refers to a
request from Lochwinnoch Club for a donation towards expenses
of the litigation (referred to in minute of 11th January 1850) forced
upon them by the Castle Semple owners.

6th November, 1851—A committee meeting held in Burns Cottage
for the purpose of raising the entry money agreed that new members
should pay ten shillings.

29th October, 1852—A general meeting was held in Mrs. Sinclair's
Curler's Tavern to elect office-bearers, etc. The following were
elected:

Jas. Gibson, Esq.	—	Patron.
Mrs. Gibson	—	Patroness.
John White, Esq.	—	President
John Smith	—	Vice-Pres.
Revd. John Calder	—	Chaplain.
John Anderson	—	Treasurer.
Jas. Borthwick	—	Secretary.

Committee—Andrew Roy, Thos. Granger, Thos. Smith, Geo.
Smellie.

William Morrison and John Rochead—Representative members.

5th November, 1852—The following new members were admitted to the Club and initiated members of the R.C.C.C.; and paid their entry money of ten shillings:

John Anderson	Mason, Partick
John Anderson	Potato merchant, Sandyford.
John Ferguson	Spirit merchant, Dumbarton Road.
William McFarlane	Byres Road.
William Campbell	Burns Cottage.
John Marshall	Old Bridge Inn.

2nd December, 1852—A committee meeting was held in the house of Mr. Wm. Campbell and resolved 'that no charge be made for strangers playing on the Partick Ice upon no account whatever, and that in the event of any member being unengaged in any game it will be lawful to take in a stranger as an opponent for the time being, provided always that, if any member wish to join in the game, the stranger must retire and allow the member to join in his stead. Also that, if any respectable party wish to play a game by themselves upon the ice, and the ice be sufficiently strong to allow such a game to take place they be allowed to do so, provided always that no stranger be allowed to go on the ice unless with the consent of one or more of the office-bearers for the time being and a majority of the members upon the ice at the time'.

This is a somewhat involved resolution. It does however show a generous spirit and a willingness to invite a stranger on the bank to join in a game, and even to give facilities for a whole rink of strangers to play a game on the Club's rink if members do not wish to play at the time.

15th February, 1853—Grand match at Carsebreck—170 rinks engaged. North win by 333 shots. John Rochead (Partick) 16, Peter Archibald (Bridge of Allan) 12.[1]

19th February, 1853—A medal competition between Partick and Chryston Clubs was played on Hogganfield Loch, 'three rinks a side of four players each. There was excellent play on both sides, and there prevailed throughout the greatest good feeling and harmony twixt the contesting rinks. Everything went on to the curlers' hearts content—nobody fell out and nobody fell in'. It was evidently a

[1] From Royal Club Annual, 1854-55.

more than usually harmonious game, which the Secretary, whose name does not appear among the players, also seems to have enjoyed. The result was:

Andrew Roy's rink	18	
John Anderson's rink	14	Chryston Total = 38
John Rochead's rink	11	
	43	(Partick 5 shots up)

18th March, 1853—At a general meeting held in the house of Mrs. Sinclair's Curler's Tavern the following members were initiated into the R.C.C.C.:

Duncan Smith, gardener, Sauchfield Cottage.
William Johnston, spirit merchant, Partick.
John Wilson, baker, Dumbarton Road, Partick.
John Smellie, of Smellie Brothers, Wrights, Partick.
James Russell, wright and builder, Franklin Terrace.
John Waddell, grocer, Dumbarton Road, Partick.
John Marshall, spirit merchant, Old Bridge, Partick.

'The above named were regularly initiated and paid their respective fees connected therewith.'

25th October, 1853—A general meeting was held in the house of Mr. Andrew Roy, Old Bridge Inn, for the purpose of electing office-bearers, etc., when the following were appointed:

James Gibson, Esq.	—	Patron
Mrs. Jas. Gibson	—	Patroness
John White, Esq.	—	President.

William Morrison and John Rochead—Representative members.

Revd. John Calder	—	Chaplain
John Brownlie	—	Treasurer
James Borthwick	—	Secretary.

Committee—James Wilson, James Bennie, Thos. Granger, George Smellie, John Anderson.

Six new members were initiated to the R.C.C.C.:

Robert Brand, Peel Terrace, Western Road.
Thomas Black, slater, Partick.
Andrew Hosie, tailor and clothier, Partick.
James Mather, baker, Old Bridge, Partick.
William Douglas, slater, Partick.
David Dick.

12th November, 1853—'died this day in Partick, John Shearer, weaver. He was ten years an officer in the Club. In his lifetime he was respected and died much lamented by all who knew him.' His name does not appear in these minutes. He must have been a curler and worthy member of the Club which undoubtedly existed before 1842.

January, 1854—The following is a list of rinks as given to Secretary:

Invincible, No. 1 —	John Anderson	Skip
Kapher, No. 2 —	Andrew Roy	,,
Bloomer, No. 3 —	Peter McGaw	,,
Calefornia, No. 4 —	Jas. Borthwick	,,

There is no further reference to these promiscuous rink names, and no further minute this season.

30th October, 1854—The annual general meeting was held in the house of William Johnston, spirit dealer, Dumbarton Road. The following office-bearers were elected:

James Gibson, Esq.	— Patron
Mrs. James Gibson	— Patroness
Peter McGaw	— President
John Smith	— Vice-President.

William Morrison and John Rochead—Representative members.

Revd. John Calder	— Chaplain
James Brownlie	— Treasurer
Thomas Granger	— Secretary.

Committee—Archd. Anderson, Jas. Russell, Andrew Roy, Thos. Smith, Adam McAulay.

During November, 1854—The following members were initiated into the R.C.C.C.:

James Gibson, spirit dealer, Glasgow.
John Campbell, spirit dealer, Partick.
James McGregor, Contractor, Partick.
John Maxwell, builder, Partick.
Hugh McConnell, bleacher, Kirklee.
William McSkimming, factor, Partick.
James Walker, baker, Partick.
James Craig, merchant, Partick.

22nd January, 1855—started a period of more or less continuous frost till well on in February. One can imagine the Secretary receiving short notice challenges from other clubs and sending out messengers to the houses and places of business of the President and the skips to lay down their professional pens and tradesmen's tools and to get their rinks arranged and curling stones, crampets, etc., ready for the fray! As these matches often took place at a distance from the burgh, and transport may not always have been easily available, the skips and players no doubt experienced some trouble arranging their affairs. However the club records make no mention of this and state 'the members had a glorious time,' which is not to be wondered at, as:

On 24th January—a number of members met this morning to play for the Rink Medal. Four rinks were drawn. Andrew Roy's rink were two shots up on Peter McGaw's after three hours keen play, and Archd. Anderson's six up on John Smith's; final, A. Roy's rink were six up on Archd. Anderson's, and declared victors for the year.

On 27th January—the annual points game was played on the Club ice. Twenty-nine players took part in eight points. Hugh Smith won with eight points, second equal J. R. Barclay and Peter McGaw, seven each.

Then followed a series of eight matches:

Date 1855		No. of Rinks	Opposing Club	Played	Result for Partick
Jan.	29	5	New Monkland	away	86 down
,,	31	1	Glasgow Victoria	home	10 up
Feb.	1	5	Cathcart	home	27 ,,
,,	3	4	Cambuslang	away	35 ,,
,,	9	5	Lennoxtown and Dumbarton	away	45 ,,
,,	12	3	Yoker	away	4 ,,
,,	20	4	Kelvindock[1]	away	34 ,,
,,	22	5	Dalry Union[1]	away	5 ,,

[1] Late in February—There is a story of these days at Clayholes. Curlers playing late in the season as they no doubt did continue casual games as long as Jack Frost obliged. The farmer came over to them asking, 'when are you b - - - - - s going to stop your games and let me get on wi' ma plooin' '.

In the series the Club rinks had a remarkable run of success, losing only the first which was for a Royal Club district medal, and when all five rinks were down. The match on 31st January was 'a friendly game against a "crack" rink of the Glasgow Victoria Club for beef and greens'. The skips in these matches were—John Anderson, Archd. Anderson, Andrew Roy; and Hugh Smith and John Smith played in five each.

On 15th February there was a Club members' game for coals for the poor in the burgh.[2] Three rinks of members East of Victoria Street met three rinks from West of said Street, and East won by 16 shots. 'With the assistance of a few friends 62 carts of coal (each of 12 cwts.) were distributed to 62 deserving families'.

On 20th July—a committee meeting appointed a sub-committee of John White and Thos. Granger to review the rules and regulations of the Club.

12th October, 1855—The annual general meeting was held in Mr. Walker's Restaurant Hall. The subscription for the present year was fixed at 4/-. The following persons were entered into membership of the Club and the R.C.C.C.:

J. R. Barclay and D. C. Barclay, Glasgow.
John Farley, spirit merchant, Partick.
William Simpson, manager of brick works, Dowanhill.
John Kemp Bruce, Glasgow.
Hugh Urquhart, Partick.

The rules and regulations drawn up by John White and Thomas Granger were read and approved and the secretary was ordered to get the same printed for distribution among the members.

The following office-bearers were appointed:

Mr. James Gibson   —   Patron
Mrs. James Gibson   —   Patroness

---

[2] 'In seasons of dearth, or of particular severity, coals and meal were occasionally played for at parish contests; and whilst the curlers were made happy over beef and greens, with a brimming bowl of whisky-punch, the church elders and officers were often employed in distributing food and elding (fuel of any kind) amongst the poorer classes.'—Dr. James Taylor's *Curling*, p. 162.

Mr. John Smith   —   Preses.
Mr. John Anderson   —   Vice Preses.
Representative members   John White and John Morrison.
Revd. John McColl   —   Chaplain
James Brownlie   —   Treasurer
Thomas Granger   —   Secretary.

Committee—Archd. Anderson, Andrew Roy, Thos. Smith, Wm. Simpson, Wm. Dickson, Wm. Douglas, and John Maxwell.

10th December—The committee met and agreed that the Rink Medal match take place on the 13th inst. commencing at 8.0 a.m. and that 2 hours be allowed for each game, 'skips not forward at that hour will be excluded'.

13th December—Five rinks met. Arch. Anderson's rink won.

21st December—The annual points game was held. Twenty-six members took part and played 8 points. The medal was gained by Wm. Douglas with 7 points, 4 members tied for 2nd place with 6 shots.

12th January, 1856—'A messenger being sent by the East Kilpatrick Club requesting the Partick Club to meet them on St. Germain's Loch to play for the District Medal awarded by the R.C.C.C. A committee meeting was called in the house of Mr. Wm. Johnston. After some discussion the committee considered it would not be doing justice to themselves to meet the East Kilpatrick people on their own ice. Hugh Miller was dispatched with their message to intimate that the Partick Club would prefer meeting them on neutral ground, and if practicable to arrange accordingly, which being agreed to, Monday the 14th was fixed on for the match to be played on the Yoker pond.'

14th January—3 rinks of the P.C.C. met an equal number of the East Kilpatrick Club. After four hours' keen play the Partick Club came off victors, by 16 shots (67-51). The Partick skips were Archd. Anderson, 2 up; And. Roy, 7 up; Adam McAulay, 7 up. The umpire Mr. Richmond handed over the medal to the Secretary, who in turn passed it to the Preses.

30th January—Challenges received from Cathcart and Kelvindock Clubs to play friendly matches on their ponds on 1st February, and accepted. Four rinks went to Cathcart, but ice was very bad and game was abandoned when score was Cathcart 49 shots, Partick 28. Skips were Wm. Simpson, Archd. Anderson, Andrew Roy and John Anderson. Three rinks played at Kelvindock. After three hours play on very bad ice, Partick finished 7 shots up (68-61). Skips were John Fairlie, William McLaws and John Smith.

Later in February—Four Partick rinks played four Gorbals Club rinks. After four hours keen play on Partick pond, the Partick rinks won by 83 shots. Skips were John Anderson, Archd. Anderson, Andrew Roy.

2nd October, 1856—A committee meeting held in the house of James Moses for the purpose of arranging to form a province with the other clubs. The secretary was instructed to write to the General Secretary of the R.C.C.C. for further information.

This reference to forming a province is the first in the Club minutes, but it was first suggested by Mr. James Ogilvie Dalgleish[1] of Abdie, one of the first vice-presidents of the Grand Club in 1846. Two years later a committee of the Royal Club, to whom consideration of the subject had been entrusted, gave an elaborate report recommending 'that the whole associated clubs, according to their locality, shall be formed into provinces, consisting of six or any greater number of clubs, according to their density in the neighbourhood, the advantage of a field of ice, and facilities for reaching it, etc.'[2]

The same committee prepared an elaborate scheme, made a classification into sixteen provinces, but recommended that it be not pressed for several reasons—expense, great increase in the Secretary's labours and some opposition from various clubs.

They left the Provinces to organise, if they wished, without the interference of the Royal Club, and give their own prizes, and appoint their own umpires 'taking care that any match which they might form should not interfere with the Grand National Match.' The representative meeting of 25th July, 1849 approved that report, and promised a district medal to such provinces as proceeded to organise on the lines of the report. As the number of provinces

[1] Kerr's *History of Curling*, pp. 265-267.
[2] About this time the number of affiliated clubs was rising rapidly. In 1838 it was 28; in 1842, 96; and by 1850 there were 243.

increased, disputes became so numerous and took up so much time at the Annual Meeting that it was resolved on the motion of Mr. Dalgleish (24th July, 1857) to give the provinces Home Rule. The resolution was to this effect—'That in Provincial matches all rules and regulations shall be arranged within the province itself, umpires and final referees appointed, and that all difficulties and disputes which may arise shall be settled within the province, and that no right of appeal to the Representative Committee of the R.C.C.C. shall be competent.'

10th October, 1856—The Annual General Meeting of the Club was held in the Masons' Lodge. The following office-bearers were elected:

James Gibson	—	Patron
Mrs. James Gibson	—	Patroness
John Anderson	—	President

John White and John Morrison—Representative members.

Revd. John McColl	—	Chaplain
James Brownlie	—	Treasurer
Thomas Granger	—	Secretary.

Committee—Archibald Anderson, Andrew Hosie, Wm. Simpson, Wm. Dickson, Wm. Douglas, John Marshall, James Moses.

Subscription to be 5/-; and a number of members not being present it was proposed that the committee take districts and call on all the absent members and intimate to them that their yearly subscription was due and unless paid by 1st November, their names would be withheld from the Annual, and, before getting the privilege of members again, they would require to enter anew.'

29th October—It being reported by John Anderson that our pond at Clayholes was likely to be let as a quarry a committee meeting was called in the house of William Furlong. Mr. John Smith said ground could be got beside the bowling green in Peel Street. A committee was appointed to deal with the matter, get estimates of the cost, and report to a meeting on Friday 31st.

31st October—A general meeting of the Club was held in Old Masons' Lodge to hear the report from the committee appointed. The reported success in getting the ground at Peel Street, estimated cost about £6, and were instructed to get the work done.

December, 1856—Committee meetings in Old Masons' Lodge initiated the following new members to the Club and to the R.C.C.C.

John McGilchrist, Robert Craig, John Dunn, James Moses, James Hodge, John Wilson, A. Auld, A. Arthur, T. Steel, A. Kerr, M. Walker, J. Black, D. Black, Jas. Fergusson, Sam McCulloch, Thos. Brown.

There was evidently no curling this season. A committee meeting on 27th April, 1857 when it was agreed to let 'the grass on the pond for grazing purposes' to Mr. Wm. Johnston at rate of £2 4s. to Martinmas 1857, the Club reserving the right to make any necessary (alteration) on the same. The small plot of ground attached was at same time let to John Anderson for the sum of 7/6d., both rents to be paid at the term of Martinmas following.

On 21st and 24th September, and on 1st and 8th October—Committee meetings were held concerning the supply of water to the new pond in Peel Street. It was not practicable to take water from the Hayburn, but a recommendation that water be taken from the old source with a filter or cesspool filled with ashes to purify the water was agreed to. Committee of three appointed to see this carried out at cost not exceeding £7.

9th October, 1857 — Annual General Meeting, held in Old Masons' Lodge. The following office-bearers were appointed:

David Tod, Esq.   — Patron
Archibald Anderson— President
William Douglas   — Vice-President.
   John White and John Anderson—Representative members.
Revd. John McColl — Chaplain
James Brownlie   — Treasurer
Thomas Granger   — Secretary.

Committee—Andrew Hosie, Wm. Simpson, John Maxwell, Jas. Moses, Andrew Roy, John Smith, Robert Barbour.

It was agreed to have a house built for holding curling stones, cost not to exceed £6. A sub-committee was appointed to take estimates and report. Also agreed that 3/- be subscription for the season, and that each member pay 2/- towards cost of stone house.

20th October—On this date the committee accepted offer of £6 to build a wooden house for curling stones. Mr. Archd. Anderson kindly offered to paint the front of the house imitation brick without charge.

29th October, 1857—Committee meeting in the shop of Archd. Anderson. The President stated he had received a letter from the Superintendent of Police complaining of the filthy state of the curling pond and ordering all nuisance to be removed in the space of 24 hours. It was decided to discontinue using the water from the old drain. Robert Barbour said corporation water would not cost more than £1 per annum, and offered to lay pipes to supply the pond and charge the Club 20 per cent a year, which was accepted. It appears they had been over-cautious in trying to save money, but did not get away with it!

19th February, 1858—Five rinks went to meet five rinks of the Old Monkland Club at Gartcosh to play for a District Medal of the Royal Club. Only four Monkland rinks turned up, so a Partick rink had to stand aside. Partick won by 14 shots.

20th February—Five rinks of the Club met this morning to compete for the Rink Medal. In the final A. Anderson's rink met J. Anderson's. The ice being in a weak condition and covered with water, J. Anderson's men were not able to play up their stones and wished the rink shortened, which was refused. A. Anderson gained the medal, J. Anderson and rink protesting.

22nd February—'William Morrison, Esq., 131, Argyle Street, Glasgow, having presented the Club with a splendid Silver Medal to be played for at points, and to become the property of the party who may win it three consecutive years. The party who may hold it for the time being to give security to Mr. John White or Mr. J. Anderson for its safe keeping.' The members met this morning to compete for the medal. Andrew Roy won with a score of ten points. 'Mr. Andrew Hosie became security for Mr. Roy producing the medal when required.'

15th October, 1858—Annual General Meeting in Old Masons' Lodge, Partick. Office-bearers appointed:

David Tod, Esq.　　— Patron
James Brownlie　　— President

The Old Partick Bell

James Moses   —   Vice-President.
John White and John Anderson—Representative members.
  Revd. John McColl   —   Chaplain
  Peter McGaw   —   Treasurer
  Thos. Granger   —   Secretary.

Committee—Archd. Anderson, A. Roy, John Smith, Thos. Smith, Robert Barbour, John Dunn, John Anderson.

Thos. Smith complained that his rink had been ill-used at the match with Old Monkland Club in having to stand-by for want of opponents.

Mr. John White suggested that, if there was to be any alteration of the rules, this was the meeting to make them. The Secretary was requested to read over the rules.

No. 3 was amended—the entrance money shall be 15/- and each member shall pay at the annual meeting the sum agreed thereat for the purposes of the Club. Any member who has not paid his yearly subscription by 31st December shall have no voice in the business of the Club, provided always he has been asked for the same, but no member shall be excluded from the Club till the following year after which he will have to pay his entry money anew.

Rule 13—when a match is to be played with any other club the committee shall appoint the skips, who shall have the power of choosing their own players.

29th November, 1858—Members of the Club met at the pond to play a match for coals for the poor; losers to pay 2/- and winners 1/- each. The President's party were the victors, and the result enabled a distribution of 24 carts to be made.

20th January, 1859—'a general meeting was held in the house of Hugh Urquhart to consider whether we should go to the county matches. Geo. Wilson moved that the Club go to the County of Lanarkshire Curling Match, and that it be voluntary for any skip to go. This was agreed and the following skips agreed to go—A. Roy, A. Anderson, John Anderson, Jas. Moses and Robert Barbour. Mr. Archd. Anderson proposed and Mr. John Fairlie seconded that the Society's Books be at all the meetings, and the minutes of former meetings read and, if approved, signed by the President.' Mr. Barbour proposed and Mr. A. Anderson seconded 'that the Secretary write to Mr. Ross that they will be happy to meet him to

B

arrange about the bell in any place he might appoint.' Messrs. A. Anderson, Barbour, J. Moses and Granger to meet Mr. Ross.

8th February, 1859—A committee meeting in the house of J. Moses to consider the forming of a province with seven other clubs. John White stated he had had some correspondence with Mr. Cassells, Secretary of the Royal Club on the subject that by forming ourselves into a province of eight clubs we would get a medal to compete for. It was agreed that the Secretary communicate with the following clubs on the subject—Vale of Leven, Dumbarton, Dumbarton Lennox, Duntocher, East Kilpatrick, Maryhill, Carbeth, and Allander or Milngavie. 'The committee appointed to confer with Mr. Ross stated that they had met him frequently but had not come to any satisfactory result.'

7th April—'Mr. Granger later saw Mr. Ross, when he promised to present the bell to the Club any day after the 19th of April.'

25th April, 1859—Committee meeting in the house of James Moses to arrange about receiving the Old Partick Bell from Mr. Ross and to initiate him into the Partick and Royal Clubs. Mr. Ross having been initiated it was proposed that we have a dinner in the Tontine Hotel (Logans) and receive the Bell there. The Secretary was instructed to write all the members that the dinner and presentation would take place on the 29th current and invite all to attend. It was also proposed that the Club pay the expenses connected with the presentation.

Tontine Hotel, 29th April, 1859—'The members of the Club and their friends sat down to dinner in the Tontine Hotel this evening. The chair was occupied by Mr. Jas. Brownlie, President, and the Croupier's chair by Mr. Jas. Moses. After the usual toasts Mr. Ross rose and in a neat speech presented the Bell mounted on a beautiful stand. The Club acknowledged the gift through their President.'

SANDYFORD, GLASGOW—*29th April*, 1859

To the President, Vice-President,
Directors and Members of the
Partick Curling Club.

Dear Sirs,
I have much pleasure in presenting your Club with the Bell which at one time was used by the Village Bellman of Partick from the date it bears

until 1779 and as its antiquity is worth respecting I present it to your Club on the conditions that it be played for yearly, the winner to retain it for the season, but he shall hand it over to the President at the next Annual General Meeting who shall keep it until his successor in office be declared, to whom it shall then be given, and that the custodiers for the time shall reside at no greater distance from the Cross of Partick, eastward than the property I now possess, namely No. 215 Dumbarton Road, Sandyford, but on no account at any time to be in the custody of any member residing on the opposite side of the Clyde from Partick, and that they shall provide two sureties of £15 each, that it will be properly and in good condition given over to the party next entitled to it, failing which the guarantee shall be realised and paid into the funds of the club, and any one member shall have the power to see that the Directors for the time being perform their part of the duty, and if at any time the club shall average less than eight members for one year the Bell shall then become the property of the Magistrates and Commissioners of the Burgh of Partick. The Directors are to be the Judges as to the best mode of playing for the Bell, and the Directors are to be the Judges of the Sureties offered by the holder of the Bell.

I am,

Yours,

Most Respectfully,

JOHN ROSS.

PARTICK—*29th April,* 1859

John Ross, Esq.,

Sir,

We, the directors of the Partick Curling Club, hereby acknowledge receipt of the Old Partick Bell, subject to the conditions with which you have accompanied it, and we beg in the name of the Club to return you our sincere thanks for the kind and honourable manner in which you have presented to us such a highly prized relic of the Byegone History of Partick.

We are, Sir,

Yours Respectfully,

JAMES BROWNLIE, President
JAMES MOSES, Vice-President
PETER McGAW, Treasurer
THOMAS GRANGER, Secretary
ARCHD. ANDERSON
JOHN DUNN
JOHN ANDERSON
   Committee or Council of
   Management.

'The President have the following gentlemen as securities for the safe keeping of the Bell—John White, Miller, Scotstoun Mills, Partick, and John Anderson, Grocer, Windsor Place, Partick.

The following is a copy of their caution—We John White and John Anderson do hereby bind and oblige ourselves under a penalty of fifteen pounds each in case of failure to see that James Brownlie, presently President of the Partick Curling Club shall deliver at the proper time and place to the committee of management of said Club the Patrick Bell and stand to be presented to him for behoof of said Club. Should he fail to do so we bind and oblige ourselves to pay the foresaid penalty into the hands of the Treasurer of said Club and that without any process or steps at law whatever. Written and signed by John White and signed by John Anderson at Partick, this twenty-eighth day of April, one thousand eight hundred and fifty-nine years.

Sgd. JOHN WHITE
JOHN ANDERSON.'

9th May, 1859—Committee meeting in the house of John Fairlie. The Secretary reported he had received favourable answers on the formation of a province from the following clubs—Vale of Leven, Dumbarton, Dumbarton Lennox, Duntocher, Maryhill, Carbeth, and Cambuslang.

13th October, 1859—At a committee meeting in the house of Hugh Urquhart the following were initiated into the Partick and Royal Clubs:

James Lillie, Rose Cottage, Partick.
William Alexander.
John Gardener, Flesher, Partick.
William Cameron, Spirit dealer, Partick.
John Muir, Spirit dealer, Partick.

14th October—The Annual General Meeting in the house of Jas. Moses. The Secretary read the minutes of the last General Meeting, which were approved. The Treasurer gave a statement of his accounts, and the subscription was agreed at 5/- for the year. The grass of the pond was let to John Smith, offered and accepted at £5 10/- to be paid half-yearly. Office-bearers elected:

William Todd, Esq.   —   Patron

Archibald Anderson   — President
John Dunn   — Vice-President.
John White and Jas. Moses re-elected Representative members.
Revd. John McColl   — Chaplain
Peter McGaw   — Treasurer
Thos. Granger   — Secretary.
Committee—John Maxwell, John Anderson, Jas. Russell, A. Roy, Andrew Hosie, John Smith, Robert Barbour.

17th October—Committee meeting at 165 Dumbarton Road, Partick, for the purpose of handing over to the President, Archd. Anderson, the Old Partick Bell, presented by John Ross, Esq., and the two District Medals won by the Club; and receiving from him security for the safe-keeping of the same. The President gave his securities which were approved of. He then presented the Club with a book to be used by the Secretary as a minute scroll-book. It was also agreed to get a box for the Secretary to hold the books, cash, accounts, etc.

25th October, 1859—Committee meeting. 'It was agreed that the Old Partick Bell should be played for in rinks, and the gaining rink to play for it among themselves—the lead and the third against the skip and the second. The rink medal to be the second prize and to be played for the same as the Bell. It was also agreed that an umpire be appointed to look after the matches.'

The Secretary was instructed to write to all the clubs agreeable to the forming of a province.

16th December, 1859—Members met this morning to play at points for the two district medals which were won by John Maxwell and Thomas Granger with 9 and 8 points respectively. The President handed a medal to each. The Club divided off under the leadership of the President and the Vice-President, four rinks each, to play for coals for the poor. Result—President won by 8 shots (49-41).

17th December—Six rinks of the Club met this morning to play for the Old Partick Bell and Rink Medal. The play went on for three days—this and the following two days—in accordance with the above agreed series of rounds and ties, and finished with a final between John White and W. Dickson, which the former won, and Jas. Moses won the Rink Medal.

22nd December—Within the house of William Cameron—a meeting was held for the purpose of handing over the Old Partick Bell to Mr. John White, who produced his securities; and the Rink Medal to James Moses.

23rd December—Four rinks of the Cathcart C.C. met four rinks of the Club on Johnston Loch to compete for a District Medal of the Royal Club. After three hours and forty minutes keen play Partick were victors by 36 shots:

J. Anderson 34 v. R. Peddie 8
A. Anderson 25 v. J. Strang 21
A. Roy   23 v. J. Biggar 13
J. Fairlie   17 v. J. Fraser 21

'Abstract from the *Daily Bulletin* of 26th December, 1859—under heading "Curliana"—"On Friday the Partick and Cathcart Curling Clubs pitted themselves against each other on Johnston Loch, Gartcosh, for a medal awarded by the Royal Caledonian Curling Club. There were four rinks each, and after keen play the Partick gained on an average 9 shots in each rink, scoring a victory by a total of 36 shots". '

28th December, 1859—Committee meeting. Secretary reported he had written to the clubs willing to join in the formation of a Province, and had called a meeting of representatives from each club in Coopers' Restaurant, 43 Jamaica Street, Glasgow on 4th January at 2.30 o'clock to arrange about first Provincial Match, draw up rules, etc.

5th January, 1860—Committee meeting in Old Masons' Lodge— A. Anderson, President, reported he had attended a meeting of the representatives from the clubs communicated with in connection with a proposed province. All expressed their willingness to join and formed a committee to draw up rules, etc.

It is of interest to note that the Club's office-bearers took a leading part in the formation of a Province, and that it was their Secretary who corresponded with the other clubs about its formation. To

John White, one of their Representative Members to the Royal Club meetings, must be given the credit for promoting this by his personal correspondence and meetings with Mr. Cassells, Secretary of the Royal Club. According to the minutes of the Tenth (Dunbartonshire) Province, this first meeting of the Representatives of the clubs in Cooper's Restaurant was attended by Vale of Leven, Dumbarton, Carbeth, Allander, Kelvindock and Partick. Notices had also been sent to Lennox Club and Duntocher, who signified in writing their desire to join.

Office-bearers were there and then appointed:

Mr. White (Partick)   —   President
Mr. Lowe (Dumbarton)   —   Treasurer
Mr. Wilson (Carbeth)   —   Secretary
Mr. Scott (Kelvindock) and Mr. Boston (Vale of Leven)—
    Council of Management
Mr. Caldwell (Wellcroft Club)   Umpire for the year.

18th January, 1860—Committee meeting in the house of James Moses, Partick. The Chairman reported he had attended committee meeting of the Province for the purpose of balloting the clubs for a Bonspiel—Partick 3 rinks drawn against Kelvindock No. 1, Lennox No. 1 and Duntocher No. 3. The committee appointed a sub-committee to arrange distribution of coals to the poor.

31st January—Andrew Roy's rink, who had won the earlier ties, met this morning to play down for the President's medal. He himself won the medal.

2nd February—On Club pond, Peel Street—six rinks met this morning to play for the Silver Medal, presented by Wm. Morrison, Esq. Ties were played on that day and on 9th February and the final on 10th February when John Anderson and Jas. Brownlie met this morning to compete single handed. After $2\frac{1}{2}$ hours keen play, John Anderson won the Medal by 22 shots to 17.

3rd February, 1860—Grand Match at Carsbreck—'The match started at noon and was prosecuted for upwards of an hour with great keen-ness, but the ice from the first was not good and early began to split and send up water. The thaw had set in and drizzling rain began to fall. Rinks were shortened once and again, and by a

little after two a considerable number of players had given up and
left the ice.'[1] Out of 148 rinks entered only 115 played, 920 players
being engaged. Result of match—South 1742 shots, North 1600—
majority for South 142. Four Partick rinks travelled to the match:

John Dunn	26 v. R. McNab, Callander	4
Archd. Anderson	12 v. A. Stewart, Drum Castle	9
James Moses	20 v. Wm. McNab, Rossie	14
Robert Barbour	— v. Lord C. Kerr, Scone and Perth	
	(did not turn up)	

The Scotsman reported of this match, 'The day was the last of
the frost or rather the first of the thaw. 148 rinks entered, but, owing
to the dubious state of the weather, 36 rinks did not turn up.
Nevertheless, very nearly 1,000 players, brought by special train.
from almost all parts of the country, entered in the competitions
Many ladies were present as spectators, including the Duchess of
Athol and party. The Dunkeld Club, it may be mentioned, came
out in great strength, 14 rinks, with the Duke's piper at their head.
The number of spectators was not less than 6000/7000, and the sight
of so great a multitude collected amid the snow covered wilds was
very striking. Of the zealous labours of the secretary, (Mr. Cassells),
pursued under disheartening difficulties, it would be superfluous to
speak.'

11th February, 1860—First Provincial Curling Match—extract
from *Glasgow Herald* and *Bulletin* of 13th February, under heading,
'Grand Provincial Curling Match—On Saturday the first match of
the recently formed Province of West Country Clubs for the
Caledonian Club medal came off on the pond at Lochburn near
Maryhill. The Province is composed of the following clubs—
Partick, Vale of Leven, Dumbarton, Lennox, Duntocher, Carbeth,
Allander, and Kelvindock—each furnishing three rinks of four men.
The day being of the choicest kind and the ice in excellent condition,
the scene altogether was of the most pleasing and animated descrip-
tion. The play throughout was such as reflected great credit on our
West Country Clubs. It continued for three hours and when brought
to a close by the signal agreed upon from the umpire, Mr. Caldwell,
the following was found to be the score:

[1] Particulars taken from description in Dr. Taylor's *Curling*, p. 318.

Vale of Leven—majority 19
Partick   „   13
Carbeth   „   4

Partick scored the greatest number of shots, but Vale of Leven gained the greatest number over their opponents.'

14th February, 1860—'Committee meeting in the house of John Fairlie, the Club having received a challenge from Kelvindock Curlers to meet them with five rinks tomorrow (Wednesday), for a friendly match at Lochburn. The meeting agreed that it would not be convenient as a great number of them had to attend the market— but we would meet them on Thursday and skips were appointed. The messenger sent to Kelvindock returned stating their players had other engagements on Thursday. The Chairman stated that, seeing we were to be disappointed at meeting Kelvindock players, he had half taken on a match with the Strathendrick Club, and, if the members present backed him he would appoint to meet them on Friday at Buchlyvie and play a friendly game for beef and greens. The meeting supported him.'

17th February, 1860—Extract from *Daily Herald* on Monday, 20th—'Partick and Strathendrick Match on Friday last—a friendly game for beef and greens was played between these clubs, three rinks aside on a pond at Bucklyvie. After three hours excellent play the curlers from Partick came off victors, the result per rink being:

Partick		*Strathendrick*	
J. Anderson	22	Simson	10
A. Anderson	27	McGregor	14
A. Roy	30	J. Stirling	16

Majority for Partick—39.'

8th March, 1860—The annual dinner was held this evening in the Old Masons' Lodge, the President in the chair and forty gentlemen present.

3rd April, 1860—Committee meeting—Mr. Anderson stated he had a letter from Mr. Baird, factor to Mr. Hamilton, instructing him to raise the rent for the pond to £7 sterling per year. This was agreed to. During this season the following were initiated into Partick and Royal Clubs:

James Craig, Spirit dealer, 151 Dumbarton Road.
Andrew White, Manager, Temple Skaterig.

1860-1865

October, 1860

THE Club had now completed eighteen years since being formally instituted by a few keen Partick curlers in 1842. During this period many important advances had been made in the organisation of the game by the Royal Club. The office-bearers of the Partick Club were not slow to take advantage of these well considered improvements. Shortly after its institution they applied to the Royal Club for affiliation, which was granted in 1849. The first mention of forming a province appears in the committee meeting of 2nd October, 1856, and this was accomplished on 5th January, 1860, at a meeting in Coopers' Restaurant, Glasgow. Another of the Royal Club's early innovations was the District Medals, for which local clubs are drawn against similar clubs in a neighbouring province or district. Each club is drawn every second year for these competitions, the winning club receiving a medal from the Royal Club on production of substantial evidence that the match was played in accordance with the rules for such matches.

Moreover the Club was greatly honoured by Mr. John Ross, who on 29th April, 1859 presented it with 'The Old Partick Bell', which is played for annually and is the most valued and highly appreciated trophy in its possession. In the following year the Club made Mr. Ross an Honorary Member.

During the next five years the following office-bearers continued in office: William Tod, Esq., of Ironbank, Partick, Patron; Mrs. William Tod, Patroness; Reverend Mr. McColl, Chaplain; John White, First Representative Member; and Peter McGaw, Treasurer. The Presidents, each holding office for one year were: John Dunn, Archibald Roy, Andrew Hosie, Thomas Granger and Robert Barbour. Vice-Presidents: Archibald Roy, R. Barbour, A. White, John Phillips, and John Anderson. The second Representative Members James Moses, Archibald Anderson and John Dunn. Thomas Granger, Secretary for three years and Andrew Hosie two years.

The Annual General Meetings were always held in October, when office-bearers were appointed, as were members of committee or council of management and the official skips. The treasurer reported on the Club's financial position and its membership. The entrance money for new members and the subscription were fixed. At this time there was always an income of £6 more or less from letting the ground round the pond for grazing to the highest bidder. This is probably the origin of the expression 'a rake off'.

It goes without saying that the Secretary and the Committee were left to settle most of the business and affairs—look after the pond and the supply of water, receive challenges from and issue the same to other clubs, and, though nothing of this appears in the minutes, arrange transport to the various places when matches were played 'away'. Almost all General and Committee meetings were held in the 'houses' of spirit dealers for want of any better place. They would be frequent or infrequent according to the prevailing weather. For instance, a committee meeting of 26th November, 1862 finishes with the additional statement—'Old Jenny Thaw, having come in search of her old man John, and having taken him away for a season, the above arrangements were of necessity done away with.'[1]

As a result of a committee meeting on 3rd June, 1861 the members found themselves included in a patriotic diversion—The Laying of the Foundation Stone of the Wallace Monument on the Abbey Craig, Stirling, on the 24th of that month. Details of this with the Secretary's minute are recorded on pp. 51-52.

October 1860-*March* 1865—New members initiated—At the annual general meeting on 16th October, 1863—Mr. William Morrison was unanimously elected as Honorary Member.

October 1860	Members as at 16th
Peter Brownlie, Saddler, Lorne Place, Glasgow	October, 1860 from R.C.
Robert Sinclair, Gas Account Collector	Annual 1860-61, page 88.
John Clark, Meadowbank Place, Partick	*Regular Members*—
Thomas Dunlop, Dairyman, Hayburn Street	John Anderson, Sen.
December 1861	John White
Thomas Barclay	John Smith
R. Thomson	Peter McGaw
John Philips	James Brownlie
George Neilson	John Harvie
John McKie	Thomas Smith
D. More, Jun.	George Smellie

[1] At a committee meeting on 10th November, 1863, 'Mr. Robert Barbour moved the following resolution that in future blindfolding of new members be done away with. It was seconded by Mr. McGaw and was unanimously carried.' (10 members present.)

William Kirkwood
J. Thomson
John Auchincloss
October 1862
A. Harkness, Spirit Dealer, Partick[1]
October 1863
Charles Morrison, Baker Argyle St., Glasgow
Robert Dickson, Spirit Merchant, Partick
John Cameron, Blacksmith, Orchard Street, Partick
Charles Smith, Argyle Arcade, Glasgow
Thomas Fletcher
C. Morrison
October 1864
James Liddel
J. B. Houston

Thomas Granger
Archd. Anderson
Andrew Roy
Hugh Smith
John Anderson, Jun.
James Russell
Andrew Hosie
William Douglas
John Fairlie
J. Maxwell
James Moses
James Hodge
J. McWaters
Robert Barbour
John Dunn
David More
David Russell
Thos. Dunlop
W. O. Watson
George Palmer
Occasional Members—
28.

The overall results of matches played and bonspiels taken part in by the Club during this period—October, 1860 to March, 1865—are very interesting and show a remarkably high average standard of success against their opponents.

Of the Grand Match at Carsbreck on 31st December, 1861 there is no mention in the minute book. We must assume the Club was not represented, which is not surprising. Dr. Taylor remarks, 'The weather was uncertain till a few hours before the start. When Mr. Cassells, Secretary of the Royal Club, went up the day before there was a sharp frost at Stirling, a decided thaw at Dunblane, and half an inch of water at Carsbreck. Matters got worse till 10 p.m. when there was a full inch of water . . . Before midnight things began

[1] Minute of Meeting 'within the house of A. Harkness, 215 Dumbarton Road, Partick, on the 30th day of October, 1862, the Committee met. Members present were Messrs. A. Roy, A. White, R. Barbour, and Thos. Granger, for the purpose of examining the treasurer's books and vouchers, which were found all correct and showing a balance in his hands of £7.3/7½d. Mr. A. Harkness, Spirit Merchant, Partick, was initiated into the Partick and R.C.C.C.'—a sitting bird caught in his nest!

to mend, by 4 a.m. there was an effective frost, and before the hour of commencement (noon) the loch presented as fine a sheet of ice as curlers ever saw, even in their dreams.'

The Grand Match of 8th January, 1864 was played on Lochwinnoch between clubs north and south of the Clyde, when five rinks from Partick took part, and were highest up club on the losing side.

A. Roy	6 shots up	v. John Boyd (Elderslie and Johnston)	
J. Anderson	16 ,, ,,	v. Thomas Jack	,,
A. Anderson	26 ,, ,,	v. J. Stirrat (Renfrewshire)	
John White	7 ,, down	v. J. Gilmour	,,
R. Thomson	6 ,, ,,	v. W. Crawford (Lochwinnoch)	

Result—South 1680 shots, North 1328; Marjority for South 352. Dr. Taylor describes the scene on a perfect day and clear ice, in his *Curling*, pp. 321-3.

The Club took a prominent part in the following Province spiels—4th January, 1861 at Lochburn. Kelvindock were declared winners after disputes concerning strangers in the Vale of Leven and Duntocher rinks, which both had much higher scores and were disqualified. From the Province minute of this match it was then suggested that the next two clubs, Helensburgh and Partick (eight and eleven down respectively) should play a friendly game next day. This took place at Helensburgh on 5th January and was reported in the *Daily Herald* of 29th January: 'Curliana—Doings of the Partick Curling Club—5th January. Four rinks from Partick met an equal number of the Helensburgh Curlers at Helensburgh, when, after a very friendly game of three hours duration the Partick was victorious by 18 shots (82-64). A plentiful repast provided by the Helensburgh players added much to the hilarity of the game.'

3rd January, 1862 at Lochburn. Partick minute is extract from *Glasgow Herald* of 11th January: 'Curliana—on Friday, 3rd January the annual match of the 10th Province, R.C.C.C. was played on Lochburn. A partial thaw having taken place the previous day, only six of the ten clubs appeared on the ice. These were Helensburgh, Allander, Yoker, East Kilpatrick, Partick and Kelvindock. After about three hours keen play, the Partick was declared the highest winning rink, having with four rinks beat their opponents by 36 shots or, on an average, 9 shots per rink. Yoker were second with 8 up average per rink.'

7th January, 1864 at Lochburn—from Province minute. Nine clubs were represented. East Kilpatrick with 3 rinks were winners having average 12¼ up per rink; Partick 4th with 4 rinks were 1¾ up per rink. Partick skips: John Anderson, Archd. Anderson, A. Roy and John White.

20th January, 1865 at Lochburn. Province minute records ten clubs were represented. Dumbarton did not all appear and did not take part.[1] Partick with 4 rinks, skipped by A. Anderson, John Anderson, R. Barbour and R. Thomson, won with average of 4 shots per rink. This was also reported in R.C. Annual 1866.

District Medal and Local Matches—1861-65

Date	Opponents	Match D. Medal Friendly	No. of rinks	Partick Result won shots up Lost shots down	Remarks
9.1.61	Hamilton	F	4	W(13-12)1	on Clyde—for 'Beef and Greens'
10.1.61	Yoker	F	3	W(58-42)16	Partick—after long and stiff game
17.1.61	Wellcroft	F	1	W(27-7)20	Partick—return match
4.1.62	Lesmahago	D.M.	4		Hamilton—opponents did not appear, partial thaw
9.2.64	Lesmahago	F	4	L(62-100)38	Lesmahago, keenly contested game
11.2.64	Whitevale	D.M.	3	W(73-34)39	Lochburn, keenly contested game
22.2.64	Maryhill	F	6	W(149-109)40	Lochburn, well contested
30.1.65	Maryhill	F	4	L(65-66)1	Ice difficult, 3 hours keen play
13.2.65	St. Vincent	F	3	W(55-42)13	St. Vincent, very friendly game
17.2.65	Pollokshaws	F	5	W(105-102)3	Pollokshaws, 'Keen play but not very friendly'
20.2.65	Kirkintilloch	F	3	W(69-45)24	Partick, very friendy game
22.2.65	Govan	F	4	W(-)5	Govan, unsatisfactory, thaw set in but finished game

The following members were skips in the above matches during seasons 1863-64 and 1864-65:

> John Anderson and Archibald Anderson—in 8 matches each
> Andrew Roy and Robert Thomson   —in 5 matches each
> John White   —in 4 matches.

---

[1] As a result of this Dumbarton in October of that year resolved to withdraw from the Province.

Club competitions for 'The Bell,' Medals, etc.

25th December, 1860—A competition, President v. Vice-President, was held at the pond for coals for the poor of the burgh. The *Glasgow Herald* reported it on 29th January, 1861 under heading 'Curliana—Doings of the Partick Curling Club'—The Presidents' rinks won. The contributions from the losers together with a handsome donation from William Tod, Esq., Patron of the Club, enabled the Club to distribute 90 carts of coal to poor households, several members offering to do the carting free.

28th December—The Rink Medal played for and won by Andrew Roy's rink.

29th December—Twenty members competed for the Points Medal, which was won by John White with 8 points.

1st January, 1862—Points Medal played-for by twenty members. William Douglas, with 14 points, won the medal presented by John Dunn.

2nd January, 1862—'Old Partick Bell Competition'—6 rinks competed—and competition abandoned on account of water on the ice.

5th January, 1864—Rink Medal—Six rinks entered—medal won by A. Anderson's rink.

24th January, 1865—'Bell' Competition—result not minuted.

11th February, 1865—Points Competition—Twenty members entered—Medal won by John Anderson, who received medal presented by Robert Barbour, President.

15th February, 1865—Rink Medal competition was not completed. At annual dinner on 10th March the three members—John Anderson, William Douglas, and Andrew Hosle—still in the competition agreed that the money collected for it be donated to the Wallace Monument Fund. A sum of £4 4/- was forwarded to the Fund Treasurer.

'After the above points game on 1st January the members divided into rinks under the President and Vice-President to play a match for coals for the poor of the Burgh. After three hours keen play the President's party came off victorious, and the Club were enabled by the subscriptions from members and a handsome donation of £5 from William Tod, Esq., Patron, to distribute 82 carts of coal.'

Concerning these times, the Revd. Dr. James Taylor, D.D., of Dolphinton in his *Curling*, published Edinburgh 1884, narrates what he describes as:

An Example of Audacious Wit

'The late Sheriff Burnett of Peebles, a worthy man and keen curler, was playing in a rink with J.H., a well known Peebles character, a stone-mason by trade, a first-class curler, but a noted river poacher. Indeed, the Sheriff had nearly every winter to send him to prison for illegal fishing. On the present occasion the poacher was skip, and the Sheriff was about to play, when the former addressed him thus: "I say, Shirra, dae ye see that stane?" "Aye, Jock," answered the Sheriff. "Ah weel, Shirra," says Jock, pointing the stone with his kowe, "just gie that ane sixty days".'

Annual dinners were held at the end of each season. Those in 1861 and 1862 in the house of William Campbell and in the Pointhouse Hotel respectively. They were well attended and enjoyed, the patriotic and Loyal toasts were given and responded to, and each wound up about 11 o'clock.

The 1863 dinner was held in the house of Robert Thomson, where 40 members and friends partook of an excellent meal. The meeting was prolonged with song and sentiment until the arrival of 'Forbes McKenzie,' when the meeting broke up after a good night's enjoyment.

The 1864 dinner. As last year this function was held in the house of Robert Thomson. Thirty-five sat down to dinner, Mr. Thomas Granger, President in the chair. After the usual speeches and toasts the company was entertained with songs and stories of an agreeable nature 'until "Forbes McKenzie" stepped in and put a stop to the enjoyment and the company broke up, sorry to part but happy to meet again on a like occasion'.

The 1865 dinner was held in the same house, thirty members present with Mr. Robert Barbour, President, in the chair. The usual toasts were given and responded to 'in the true and curlers' spirit', and were followed by excellent songs and stories. As the points game for the Gold Medal was not completed, the three members who tied agreed to allow the amount subscribed to go to the fund for the 'Wallace Memorial'. The three members—John Anderson, William Douglas, and Andrew Hosie received a hearty vote of thanks from Bailie John White, who suggested a further contribution. As a result the sum of £4 4/- was sent to the treasurer of the Memorial. After a very happy evening the company was obliged to retire when 'Forbes McKenzie' made his appearance at 11 o'clock.

Wallace Monument—Laying Foundation Stone—24th June, 1861

Partick Curling Club minute 3rd June, 1861—Within the house of James Mason, spirit merchant, the committee met to consider an invitation from the Secretary of the Wallace Testimonial for as many of the Club as found it convenient to attend on the occasion of laying the Foundation Stone of the Wallace Monument on Abbey Craig.

The Secretary was requested to write to the members asking them and giving them an opportunity to attend same as a club. The Secretary (Thomas Granger) evidently did so in persuasive and patriotic terms, as the following minute of their day in Stirling so forcibly and rhetorically describes. He seems to have been quite carried away by the exuberant patriotism of the large company in the procession and the overflowing romanticism of the lookers-on.

'In the King's Park at Stirling on the 24th of June, 1861, about thirty members of the Club gathered and formed part of the procession of all denominations of their countrymen to march to the Abbey Craig, there to honour by their presence the name of their departed Patriot, The Noble Sir William Wallace, "The Hero of Auld Scotland," whose name was to the English as the Breath of the deadly "Simoon" is to he Arab, or the Ravenous Wolf to the Russian or Lapland travellers, by lending a helping hand in the laying of a foundation stone of a monument to be erected on the Abbey Craig to his memory as a token of the high estimation in which his countrymen hold his departed worth, and as a remembrancer in all time coming of him who so nobly has gone before, being a tribute of respect so dearly won by him, who suffered death rather than submit to the "Power Seeking" English, or prove a

Knave to his Country. The curlers were rallied round their handsome
Silken Banner, presented to the Club by Mr. John Dunn and
crowned by an imitation Curling stone presented by Mr. John White.
The Partick Curling Club formed no mean part of the lengthy
procession. The whole proceedings passed off with complete success, and the curlers then wended their way home, no doubt much
pleased and much edified by their journey north.'

Excerpts from the *Glasgow Herald*, Tuesday, 25th June, 1861.
The paper gave a very full description of the day's events, and a
leading article with caustic references to the long time taken to raise
the necessary money.

'The grand procession to the Abbey Craig commenced to form
in the King's Park at 12 noon, and shortly after one o'clock it began
to move . . . and could not have consisted of less than 8/10,000
individuals . . . led by two horsemen in ancient armour, followed by
Lt. General Sir James Maxwell Wallace, K.C.B., the Deputy Grand
Marshall, and a band. Then seventeen companies of volunteers,
each representing its volunteer regiment . . . These were succeeded
by the Curlers consisting of representatives of the Clubs of
Cardross, Cambuslang, Partick, Strathendrick, Port of Menteith,
from the Clyde and Lennox areas; and of representatives of
twelve other clubs from other parts of Scotland, interspersed with
various pipers. Gardeners' Lodges followed and the Oddfellows'
Societies, Municipal bodies from all parts including Inverness,
Ayr, Musselburgh and Dumbarton, the last preceded by the Master
Gunner of Dumbarton Castle, bearing the sword of Sir William
Wallace. The Wallace Committee and speakers came next and
were followed by Masonic Lodges. The Masonic formalities and
speech-making at the Abbey Craig followed. In the evening a banquet was held in Stirling, followed by many more speeches. It
was a general holiday all over the surrounding districts.'

1865-1870

DURING the next five seasons—October 1865 to March 1870—a noteworthy event was that the club decided in January, 1867 to honour its worthy and esteemed Patron, William Tod, Esq., of Ayton, by presenting to him a pair of curling stones as a small token of its esteem and appreciation of his continued interest and generosity to the club over many years. This was done, but, to the great regret of all the members, Mr. Tod died before the presentation took place. The stones were thereafter sent to Mrs. Tod, who graciously thanked the club for the 'very beautiful stones, and said they would be as much prized by her as they would have been by him'. At the following Annual General Meeting on 11th October of that year the club unanimously agreed that Mr. David Tod of Ironbank, Partick, be invited to act as patron. In due course Mr. Tod thanked the club for the honour thus conferred upon him and had pleasure in accepting. At this same Annual General Meeting in October, 1867 Mr. John White proposed and Mr. Archibald Anderson seconded 'that we cease to have connection with the Lanarkshire (Province) Club'. This was unanimously agreed.

Curling matches during this quinquennial period were confined to the month of January, 1867 and a few days in the winter of 1869–70. A committee meeting of 26th December, 1867 states 'There was no business before the committee, but a strong desire that Jack Frost would favour us with his presence as early as possible.' They were so favoured, as during the following month they had the province Bonspiel, 3 District Medal and 3 inter-club matches, a points game, and played for coals for the poor.

The following office bearers held office:

Patrons and patronesses—1865–1867—Mr. and Mrs. William Tod
of Ayton.
1867–1870—Mr. and Mrs. David Tod of
Ironbank.

Presidents—Thomas Smith, John McGilchrist, John Phillips, John
Maxwell and John Clark.

Vice-Pres.—John McGilchrist, Peter Brownlie (2), William Douglas,
Jas. Millar.

Chaplain—Rev. John McColl (five years).

Representative members—John White (five), Archibald Anderson (two), John Anderson (three).

Treasurer—Peter McGaw, Thos. Granger, Thos. Smith (three).

Secretary—A. Hosie (four), Arch. Anderson.

New members admitted—

1865-66	**1866-67**	**1867-68**
James McBride	John Phillips	Peter Struthers
William McGavin	Duncan Campbell	George Thomson
James White	George Mathewson	R. Waddell
William Arthur	Peter McGaw, Junr.	J. Marshall
Robert Carrick	James Perry	John Russell
Robert Anderson		James Austan
R. Samuels	**1869-70**	John Orr
	Wilfred Robertson	James Wilkie
1868-69		
James Bruce		

Bonspiels

There were no Grand Matches[1] during this period and only one xth Province Bonspiel—on 14th January, 1867 at Lochburn for an R.C.C.C. Province Medal. Twenty-one heads were played on 'First Quality Ice'. All clubs were represented, except Dumbarton which had in October 1866 resolved to withdraw from the Province. The result taken from the Province minute:

Partick with 4 rinks—40 shots up $= 12\frac{1}{2}$ average
Carbeth	,,	3	,,	35	,,	,,	$= 11\frac{2}{3}$	,,
Kelvindock	4	,,	13	,,	,,		$= 3\frac{1}{4}$	,,
Cardross	2	,,	5	,,	,,		$= 2\frac{1}{2}$	,,
Yoker	,,	2	,,	1	,,	,,	$= \frac{1}{2}$	,,

Allander, Helensburgh, Duntocher and East Kilpartick were down. Partick winners, were represented by:

John Anderson	21 shots	v. J. Edgar	21
John White	24 ,,	v. J. Gray, Yoker	14
Arch. Anderson	30 ,,	v. – Brison, Old Kilpatrick	12
Robert Thomson	32 ,,	v. – Brown	10

[1] This is not correct. There was a Grand Match at Carsbreck on 15th January, 1867—133 rinks—Majority for South 103 shots.

Date	Match D. Medal F. Friendly	No. of rinks	Result for Partick Win or Loss	Opponents, Place and Remarks
3. 1.67	F.	3¹	W (73-65)	St. Vincent, Partick, day and ice good, greatest friendship prevailed.
4. 1.67	D.	4¹	W (88-54)	At Lochwinnoch, keen and clear, exciting contest.
11. 1.67	F.	4	W (82-56)	Kelvindock, Lochburn, kindliest feeling prevailed.
12. 1.67	D.	4¹	W (96-55)	Boreas, Paisley, Partick, keenly contested.
18. 1.67	F.	4¹	L (77-78)	Pollokshaws, Partick, keenly contested.
21. 1.67	D.	4¹	W (82-61)	Cambuslang, keen contest throughout.
7.12.69	D.	3		Abandoned—rain and water—replayed.
27.12.69	replay	3¹	W (65-45)	
22. 2.70	F.	3	W (67-59)	At Carbeth—'most beautiful sheet of ice, inviting a second game, in which the Partick Club was again victorious. Afterwards Jas. Gilchrist, Esq., Carbeth, kindly invited the Partick Curlers to tea which was highly appreciated'.

Club Games (*Points*): On 13th January, 1867, twenty-seven members contested for the Points Medal. Thos. Smith won the extra ends after a tie with Arch. Anderson of 8 points each. There were games for coals for the poor on 21st February, 1866 and 5th January, 1867, 'three hours keen play', but no other details. On 4th Dec., 1869 the weather not being favourable 'there was not our usual turn-out. However there was collected from the members and friends, including £2 2/- from our Patron, David Tod, Esq., £4 14/-.'

Annual Dinners

1866—on 22nd February in Mr. Urquhart's New Hall when 32 members and friends sat down. Mr. Thomas Smith, President, occupied the chair and was supported on the platform by Mr. William Morrison, Honorary member. The Croupier was Andrew Hosie supported by J. Ross, Honorary member. The President in his very neat and eloquent speech remarked it had been a source of great grief to him that we had not had more ice. The usual toasts were followed with excellent songs and stories, and the company broke up 'at a very reasonable² hour'.

1867—on 1st March in St. Mary's Hall, Windsor Place. The President, John McGilchrist presided over a company of forty-two. In his neat and fluent speech he recalled a good and successful

¹ In these six games John Anderson and Archibald Anderson skipped in all, Robert Thomson in 4, Robert Barbour in 3, and John White, David More and John Thomson in 1 each.

² This is correct, the minute is not 'reasonable'.

season for the club 'taking a little credit to himself in providing a larger supply of ice than our former president'!

1868—on 6th March in Mr. Robert Thomson's—thirty members and friends present. The President, John Phillips, in the chair, remarked he was exceedingly sorry that John Frost had given them so little opportunity of showing what the club, he had the honour of presiding over, was able to do. Toasts, song and sentiment followed till it was time to separate, all parting in the best of friendship.

1869—on 6th April in the house of Arch. Harkness, spirit merchant, 213 Dumbarton Road, twenty-four members and friends were present. In the absence of the President (Mr. Maxwell) and of the Secretary (Mr. Hosie) Mr. Phillips was asked to take the chair. He stated that there had been 'naw ice'. The company spent a pleasant evening 'till Forbes[1] arrived, when all separated'.

1870—on 4th March, in Robert Thomson's, 361 Dumbarton Road. Nineteen members present, and, in the unavoidable absence of the president, John Clark, John Anderson, Father of the club, was called to the chair. He congratulated members on the success of the season, and 'in the midst of our pleasures, we had not forgotten to cheer the hearts of the widow and orphan by distributing about 30 carts of coal to the poor of Partick'. A very happy evening terminated at a late hour.

[1] 'Forbes MacKenzie' re-appears after some years!

1870-1880

WE now come to the ten seasons from October 1871 to March 1880, during which the pond was moved twice, and there was little or no ice for several seasons. In the competitive matches at Bonspiels, and with other clubs for Royal Club District Medals, and in 'friendly games' the club rinks maintained a notable record of successful results.

Important events on the fringe of the Burgh were the erection of the Kibble Palace in the Botanic Gardens, and the initiation of horse-drawn trams in Glasgow on the route from the top of Byres Road at Botanic Gardens to Dennistoun.

Office-bearers—Patron and Patroness—Mr. and Mrs. David Tod of Ironbank till 1877, when they left the Burgh; and thereafter Mr. and Mrs. Hugh Kennedy.

	Presidents	*Vice-Presidents*
1870-71	John Thomson	John Auchincloss
1871-72	John Auchincloss	David More
1872-73	David More	William Kirkwood
1873-74	William Kirkwood	Duncan Campbell
1874-75	Duncan Campbell	John Maxwell, Junr.
1875-76	Thos. Fletcher	James White
1876-77	James White	R. D. Samuels
1877-78		
1878-79	John Orr	John Stewart
1879-80	William Frame	John Stewart

The Representative members John White and John Anderson remained in office during the period, as did the Chaplain, the Rev. John McColl, and the Secretary Archibald Anderson. Thomas Smith was Treasurer till he retired in 1876, and was succeeded by Duncan Campbell and Andrew Brunton. Honorary members— David Tod, Hugh Kennedy, Rev. J. McColl, and William Morrison. Ordinary members as at 16th October 1870:

John Anderson	Thos. Dunlop	James White
John White	John Phillips	Robert Carrick
Thos. Granger	Geo. Neilson	D. Campbell

Arch. Anderson	David More	G. Mathieson
Thos. Smith	Wm. Kirkwood	R. D. Samuels
Wm. Douglas	John Thomason	Robt. Waddell
J. Maxwell, Sen.	J. Auchincloss	John Orr
Robert Barbour	Thos. Fletcher	J. Maxwell, Junr.
J. McGilchrist	Wm. McGavin	A. Anderson, Junr.
Chas. Morrison	James Perry	

Occasional members—23.

During this decade the Annual General Meetings as usual were held early October when the above were appointed office bearers. The first of these A.G.M's on 14th October 1870 was held in Mr. Hugh Urquhart's Hall, Dumbarton Road, the minute of which concludes with one of the Secretary's typical notes: 'The President and Vice-President then ordered sum refreshment which afterwards brought out both song and sentiment and terminated a veary hapy meeting'—Shortly after the A.G.M's there were the usual committee meetings, when the new President, having given the usual security, received the Bell, Banner, Medals and Casket. These meetings usually concluded with the President inviting the committee to supper—'a beutful Scottish Haggis, etc., wase dawn ample justes to and a veary happy eving spent'.

1873—On 12th March the committee met—after other business it appointed a sub-committee to distribute coals to the poor and money collected by the club, including a donation of two guineas from Mr. Tod, Patron. Mr. Archibald Anderson, in name of himself and the other three in his rink—John Maxwell, Sen., David More, and John Maxwell, Junr.—who, having played against and won versus a rink at Kirkcudbright for two loads of meal, handed same over to the committee. It was then agreed to put all the money collected by the club into meal for distribution to the most deserving poor. Mr. James White then said that not only the committee, but the club, would award these gentlemen a hearty vote of thanks for their kindness in not only risking their money to go so far from home to play, but for their handing over the winnings to the club—the same to be minuted.

1875—In February a communication was received from the Royal Club asking if we would care to contribute to a testimonial to Mr. Alexander Cassels, W.S., who was retiring. (He had been

Vice-President 1843-44, Secretary 1844-46, and Secretary and Treasurer 1846-76.) The committee agreed to subscribe £3.[1]

On 12th May of this year at a committee meeting—Mr. Campbell, President in the chair, said it had been mentioned for some time past we should give Mr. Smith some recognition for his long service as Treasurer to the club, and a committee was appointed to carry out the unanimous decision.

It was arranged to present a marble clock and two bronze figures to Mr. Smith and 'Broc' ear-rings to Mrs. Smith. The presentation by Mr. Campbell, President, took place on 31st May in Mr. Anderson's house.

In September 1876—it was agreed to accept the offer of Mr. Burns, a tenant of the Railway company holding the ground where the pond was situated, of a five year lease of £7 10s. yearly; in November it was agreed to add eight feet to the clubhouse and to put it in good condition.

On 13th November 1876—A committee meeting was held in Mr. Arch. Anderson's house, John White, Pres. in the chair. After other business the President made reference to the recent death of Mr. John Clark as being an old member and at one time President, and stated that Mr. Alexander had called on him and asked him to intimate that he wished to make a present of Mr. Clark's new stones and handles, to be played for by the club.

1878—January 9th—The committee considered a letter received from the Sir Colin Campbell Curling Club,[2] regarding an extraordinary Law Action in the Court of Session against three of their members for removing their Curling Stone House at Johnston Loch, Gartcosh. The case was decided against them and they had to pay damages and expenses amounting to £229 8s. 3d. The Secretary

[1] At the Annual General Meeting of the Royal Club in the Cafe Royal Hotel, Edinburgh, on 27th July of the same year a special resolution was unanimously passed re the death of Mr. Cassels which had taken place before the handsome testimonial, of which he had been informed, had been presented. The Royal Club record of the resolution states 'we recognise, moreover, not only the keen curler, but the honourable man of business, the genial companion and the faithful citizen'.

[2] The Sir Colin Campbell Club was instituted and admitted to the Royal Club in 1855 and had 24 regular members and 16 occasional members at this time.

was instructed to ask for further information. A general meeting was held on 14th March to consider the further letter from the Sir Colin Campbell Club and after a vote between sending a donation of £5 and doing nothing, it was decided by 6 votes to 5 to send £5, which was done, at the following Annual General Meeting in October the Secretary said, with reference to this, that 'we were proud to say we were able to help our Sir Colin Campbell friends'.

1878—October—The Committee met to consider a Circular Letter 'received from the "Glaciarium", Southport, inviting curlers from all over the country to compete for a silver cup, value 25 guineas, to become the absolute property of the winners'. The Secretary was instructed to reply 'that we disapprove of curling by points and therefore decline to take part . . . If however you should adopt the system of playing by rinks, I have no doubt the Partick Club will be happy to send a rink".'

At the A.G.M. on 29th September 1879, William Frame, President in the chair—Mr. Brunton made feeling remarks on the loss the club had sustained by the deaths of Mr. William Kirkwood nad Mr. William Boag.

During this period all new members were initiated to the Royal Club by 'My Lord' John White who officiated at the Club courts and ceremonies.

It was probably about this period when the following incident took place. It is recorded in the Rev. Dr. James Taylor's 'Curling', published Edinburgh 1884. He heads it:

A Good Curler's Funeral Sermon

The late Re. Dr. Aiton of Dolphinton, an eccentric and humerous clergyman of the old school, had occasion to preach a funeral sermon on one of his elders, a keen curler like himself. In performing this duty, after enumerating how the deceased member of session among other accomplishments could 'dra a shot' on the ice or 'strike at a winner', etc., he concluded his eulogium in the following words: 'But now, my friends, he is o'er the hog-score, he's within the inner circle of eternity, and dead-guarded'.

Grand Match 26th January, 1871—at Carsbreck—112 rinks. —no rink from Partick.

Grand Match—12th February, 1873—The club was not represented.

Grand Match—24th December, 1874—The club was not represented.

Grand Match—13th December, 1878—at Lochwinnoch—between North and South of the Clyde. Partick skips—John Anderson, Arch. Anderson, D. More, William Kirkwood and Wm. Frame—scored 75 shots against their opponents from Lilybank Club, who, being in Glasgow, Lanarkshire were for the south. South won the match by 105 shots (1098-993) (from R.C. Annual 1879-80).

Grand Match—23rd January, 1880—at Carsbreck—Partick represented by 5 rinks—skips John Anderson, Arch. Anderson, James White, J. Maxwell and R. Martin—drawn against 4 Aberfeldy rinks headed by Lord Breadalbane, and one rink from Fettercairn. Partick rinks won against their opponents by 26 shots (112-86). The match ended in a win for the North by 28 shots (2830-2802), 330 rinks taking part in the match.

Tenth Province Bonspiels

29th December 1870—at Carbeth Loch— the four Partick rinks had close games with their opponents, scoring 69 to their adversaries' 68. The Partick skips were J. Anderson, A. Anderson, J. Thomson and D. More. Dumbarton and Helensburgh tied with $10\frac{1}{3}$ average up per rink, and Allander next $1\frac{2}{3}$ up. In the replay Helensburgh won by 33 up.

8th February 1873—at Loch Ardinning—Partick represented by three rinks skipped by William Kirkwood, D. More and Arch. Anderson. Kelvindock were winners with 15 shots up, Carbeth second 13, Helensburgh third 12 up, Cardross with 8, all with three rinks. Six clubs were down—Dumbarton, Partick, East Kilpatrick, Strathendrick, Allander and Duntocher.

17th December 1874—at Dougalston Loch—11 clubs represented—four rinks from Partick skipped by John Anderson, Arch. Anderson, D. More and Kirkwood. They scored 104 shots against their opponents 38, a majority of 16 up per rink and won the medal.

12th December 1878—at Loch Ardinning—eight clubs appeared[1] —Helensburgh with four rinks won with $14\frac{1}{2}$ shots up average. Yoker second with $5\frac{1}{3}$ and Partick third with $5\frac{1}{3}$. The Partick skips were—John Anderson, Arch. Anderson, D. More and Wm. Kirkwood. (Province Minute).

---

[1] 'There was a heavy fall of snow the previous night. Cardross, East Kilpatrick and Strathendrick Clubs did not appear, but the eight which did, enjoyed a splendid day's sport.'

4th December 1879—at Loch Ardinning—'Ice first class'—
Helensburgh with four rinks won with 8½ shots up per rink, Yoker
3 rinks second with 3⅓, and Partick five rinks 1⅛.   Partick skips
Wm. Frame, J. Anderson, A. Anderson, David More and Jas.
White.   There were five losing clubs (Province Minute).

District Medal and Local Matches

Date	Match D. Medal F. Friendly	No. of Rinks	Result for Partick Win or Loss	Opponents, Place and Remarks
28.12.70	D.	4	W (84-66)	Bridgeton.
25. 1.71	D.	4	L (47-94)	Strathaven, three hours' play.
26. 1.71	F.	3	W (72-43)	Kirkintilloch, Antermony L., 'Tatties and Herring'.
1. 2.71	F.	4	W (91-60)	Govan, at Partick, 'Tatties and Herring'.
16.12.74	D.	3	W (70-48)	Whitevale, at Partick, 21 heads[1].
21.12.74	D.	3	W (68-49)	Uddingston, at Partick, 21 heads[2].
11.12.78	D.	3	W (31-20)	Vale of Leven, at Partick (T. Edgar umpire), ice good.
18.12.78	F.	4	L (51-66)	Lochwinnoch, on Castle Semple Loch.
20.12.78	F.	4	W (69-40)	Govan, at Partick.
26.12.78	F.	3	W (71-34)	Yoker, at Yoker.
27.12.78	F.	4	W (111-49)	Kirkintilloch, at Partick.
6. 1.79	F.	4	W (89-79)	Maryhill, at Partick.
25. 1.79	F.	3	W (70-48)	Gourock, at Gourock.
1. 2.79	F.	3	W (64-45)	Kilmaronock, Loch Lomond.
29. 1.79	F.	4	W (73-66)	Lillybank, Lillybank ice.
11.12.79	F.	2	W (45-26)	Govan, at Partick, 'first class ice'.
12.12.79	F.	5	L (79-110)	Lillybank, at Partick.
26. 1.80	F.	4	W (73-55)	Kirkintilloch, Antermony Loch.

In the above matches Archibald Anderson skipped in 14, D.
More and John Anderson in 13 each, W. Frame 5, J. Thomson and
W. Kirkwood 3 each and John Maxwell 1.

Club Competitions for The Bell, Medals, etc.

28th January 1871—The annual game for coals to the poor of
Partick was played when a very handsome sum was collected,
including two guineas from the Patron, Mr. D. Tod, and a donation
of six tons of coal from an anonymous donor.

1874—during December—Ex-President D. More's prize was
played for—Six rinks entered and played in three ties—final John
Anderson was 4 up on W. Kirkwood.   The Bell and the Rink
Medal were also played this month, but the final between D. More
and A. Anderson never was played as the weather took a change.

7th January 1875—A committee meeting arranged the distribution of coals to the poor with donations including three guineas
from Mr. Tod.   There is no mention of the usual game for this
purpose.

[1] R.C. Annual, 1875-76—William Caldwell, umpire; 'ice first class'.
[2] R.C. Annual, 1875-76—William Caldwell, umpire; 'all that a curler could wish'.

8th December 1875—Seven rinks turned out to play for the 'Old Partick Bell' and Rink Medal. Fifteen heads were played—John Anderson's rink won the Bell and Arch. Anderson's the Rink Medal.

19th December 1878—Points game for Mr. Alexander of Clarkfield prize of the late Ex-President's new stones and handles—played on points and won by Arch. Anderson with 10.

24th December 1878—Points competion for Ex-Pres. William Kirkwood's prize for which 18 members entered, R. D. Samuels won with 10 points.

25th December 1878—Ex-Pres. D. Campbell's prize, competed for by rinks, won by Arch. Anderson with Thos. Dunlop, John Phillips and Thos Fletcher.

4th January 1879—Points competion for Ex-Pres. Jas. White's prize. Twenty-one members entered and it was won by John Anderson with a score of 17 points—the highest points score in the club.

10th January 1879—Ex-Pres. R. D. Samuel's prize—five rinks entered, won by the same Arch. Anderson rink as above.

There are also two other prizes mentioned in this season's minutes. Mr. Dart's prize of Curling Stones and Handles and Fletcher's prize, but the pencil notes are somewhat illegible.

21st January 1880—The Bell and Rink Medal Competition took place, only four rinks entered. John Anderson won the Bell and Wm. Frame the Rink Medal.

Annual Dinners

17th February 1871—The *North British Daily Mail* reported— 'The Annual Dinner of the Partick Curling Club was held when thirty gentlemen attended. Mr. John Thomson, President in the chair, with Mr. Archibald Anderson as Croupier. The usual loyal and patriotic toasts were proposed and responded to.'

1872—The dinner was arranged to take place on 1st March, but there is no minute of it

1873—The function was to be held on 8th March. A later minute of 20th March postponed 'our annual supper', as members seemed to be otherwise engaged. The supper apparently did not take place.

1874—There is no mention of any ice or play during this season, nor any mention of a dinner.

1875—There is no mention of this function on 9th March, but the *Partick Advertiser* under heading 'Partick Curling Club Dinner' reported 'The annual dinner of this club took place in the Old Masonic Lodge Hall, Dumbarton Road, and was attended by a large gathering of members and friends. Mr. Duncan Campbell, President, occupied the chair and was supported by Messrs. Thomson, Granger and Risk. After the usual loyal and patriotic toasts the chairman gave the toast of the evening—"The Partick Curling Club" . . . other toasts followed including "Royal Caledonian and kindred clubs" and commercial interests of Partick. The company broke up after spending a very enjoyable evening'.

1876—A very brief minute records the dinner was held on 21st March, when about seventy gentlemen sat down; Mr. Fletcher, President, in the chair and Mr. James White, Croupier. The *Partick Advertiser* of 25th March reported the function very fully under heading 'Curling Club Dinner'. 'The Annual Dinner of this ancient club took place on Tuesday evening in the Old Masonic Hall, Dumbarton Road . . . The Chairman was surrounded by Commissioner Trotter, Messrs. James Young, A. Marshall and W. Barr (Govan) . . . after the usual loyal toasts, "The Army, Navy, and Reserve Forces" was given and responded to by Mr. George Ward and Mr. William White. In proposing the toast of the Partick Curling Club Mr. William Barr, Govan, referred to the pleasure he and the other curlers of Govan had in fraternising with their brethren of Partick . . . the two clubs had always been very obliging to one another, and he begged to thank the Partick Club for their kindness last season in giving them the use of their pond, when the Govan one was not in condition for playing on.' Many other toasts followed, during the evening songs were numerous and the company separated at an early hour.

1877—Dinner arranged for 8th March was cancelled by a committee meeting on 5th March.

1878—On 21st March the dinner was held in Mr. McLellan's Hall, when thirty members and friends were present with Mr. Samuels, President, in the chair. He remarked that, having had no ice, we could not boast of any new victories. The minute records a very happy evening, 'with the hope of John Frost being more liberal to us next season.'

1879—On 6th February the annual dinner took place in the Lesser

Town Hall, President John Orr in the chair, and ex-president
Fletcher, Croupier. 'between forty and fifty members and friends
spent a merry evening in fighting their old battles over again.'

As, during the season the club had played nine friendly matches
with neighbouring clubs, of which they won 8, this minute modestly
makes no mention of such success—perhaps this first dinner in the
precincts of the Town Hall curbed their style a bit.

1880—A committee meeting on 12th February agreed to the
dinner being held on 4th March in the Lesser Town Hall. There
is no minute, though there are some pencilled notes of expenses
incurred therewith.

'The Partick Advertiser'

This weekly paper had a very short life from 27th February 1875
to June 24th 1876 and was printed and published in Partick for the
proprietor by John Thomlinson, Jun., 142 Dumbarton Road.

As there is no club minute of the dinner on 9th March 1875 and
that of the dinner on 21st March 1876 was very brief we have been
fortunate in finding in its pages full reports of these functions.
These have been entered in the record of minutes for these years.

In his leading articles the Editor embarked on topical talking
subjects, which he freely interspersed with Latin and French
quotations, and which provoked many readers to write letters to
him. Such articles as 'Merchants and Shopkeepers', 'The Girl of
the Period', 'The Young Men of the Period', produced some acri-
monious correspondence. There was also a demand from readers
for a public library, and a move towards co-operative societies.

One or two excerpts having reference to people and places connected with the club are of interest. The Editor's leading article in
the first issue reads 'It has been a long felt want in Partick—a
medium through which all local matters might be conveyed to the
general public, bringing before their notice what really has been
transpiring during the week, thereby aiding to diffuse a local interest
among the inhabitants. It has also been a want—a medium
whereby the public may see what is occurring in the way of cheap
sales, or where to go and buy a pair of cheap boots or a good loaf,
which is a very important question now-a-days, and which can be
answered by such an organ as the one now issued. It shall be our
earnest endeavour to continually keep the public well posted up in
local matters so that all may be able, for the small sum of one half
penny, to have a general knowledge of local affairs' . . .

This number also contains a facetious article on 'Music in Partick' and 'A Tradition of the Last Century'—a love story of the son of a ploughman named William Purdon in Bannockhill Farmhouse and Jeannie the daughter of James Scott who resided in the Knowe. Our interest in this is that in September, 1857, when the pond at Peel Street was being prepared, the Hayburn was considered as a possible supply of water, but was later found to be impracticable. The name of the farmer in Bannockhill at the time of the story was John Hayburn, whose farm buildings and fields lay on the ground sloping down from Broomhill Cross to the Hayburn. In the map of the environs of Glasgow, 1795, by Thomas Richardson, Land Surveyor, Glasgow, the Hayburn is referred to as Hay's Burn. Is it possible that in the course of years local people adopted the farmer's name when referring to the burn, and that thereafter the name of the farm was forgotten as the town began to encroach on its fields?

In the issue of 29th May 1875, under Local News—'The Academy —on Wednesday the annual exhibition of this excellent institution took place, David Tod, Esq., presided; and there was a numerous attendance of parents, guardians and friends, and of the local clergy, the Rev. Messrs. Anderson, McColl, and Grant . . . towards the close Mr. Tod presented handsome prizes to the successful pupils and in conclusion congratulated the whole of the teachers on the marked progress which had been made in the Academy during the year.' Mr. Tod was at the time Patron of the Club, and Mr. McColl, Chaplain.

A few other paragraphs from the editorial leaders and pages of this weekly newspaper furnish backgrounds, grave or gay as one chooses to interpret them, to contemporary life in the rapidly extending burgh. The paper was, as it's name implies, an advertising medium and contained announcements of many local merchants and tradesmen many of whose names were well known until recent times and including a few still in the Directory.

In No. 3 dated 13th March 1875, among notices on page one, is 'Tresspass Notice—all persons found, on or after this date, tresspassing (with or without clothes) on any of the fields at Stewartville, will be prosecuted.' In April a leading article asks 'what shall we drink'—and quotes 'chacun à son goût.' After dealing with beer (Bass and Allsop), London Porter and Dublin Stout, port and sherry —'The votaries of whisky, brandy, etc., have, we may allow, much on their side, as no doubt pure spirits, well diluted with water (by the purchaser, not the vendor) has its advantages over a questionable wine—but moderation in everything.' Issue No. 11 of 8th May the article is headed 'Veiled in a cloud of fragrance—This is what, doubtless, not a few of our readers will be when reading the Partick Advertiser. They will be enjoying what some call the "fragrant" and others the "noxious" weed. It may be as a cigar or in a meerschaum, or a common clay and it may be accompanied or not by a glass of wine, or some of the wine of the country, properly diluted with Loch Katrine . . . In ranking ourselves among the advocates for smoking, it must be with the qualification of moderation, as we have seen often enough the baneful effects of excess. Those boys whom you see with pipes in their mouths, and cheap "cabbages", may possibly rue it some day. They certainly do not require to be soothed. Time enough for them when, after a hard day's work, manual or mental, or both, they may be entitled to smoke when reading the *Partick Advertiser*— not to 11, present issue but No. 1000.' At the same time the following advert. appears: 'J. McIndoe, Tobacconist, 315 Dumbarton Road (opposite foot of Hamilton Street)—Best cut Cavendish 4d. per oz., finest smoking mixture 4½d., splendid Thick Roll Tobacco 3d., Cigars, Briar Root, and Meerschaum Pipes, Tobacco Pouches; Best Matches 3½d. per dozen.'

The writer acknowledges with thanks his obligation to Mr. John McC. Russell, C.A., for perusal of his bound copy of *The Partick Advertiser*.

C

1880-1890

THIS period was not one of hard winters, though there were four grand matches, in one of which Partick was not represented, and two inter-province bonspiels both at Lochwinnoch between Lanarkshire and Renfrewshire; and the Dunbartonshire (Tenth) Province held five bonspiels. Matches for District Medals and friendly games with neighbouring clubs were nineteen in number, of which Partick won thirteen—a very satisfactory proportion. The Annual General and committee meetings show that the office bearers were alert to all matters concerning the welfare of the club and its members. The entry money for new members remained at 10/- and the annual subscription was raised from 5/- to 7/6d. in 1881. During the summer of 1882 the water supply to the pond was not satisfactory and the question of a new pond was even considered, but in November it was agreed to puddle the pond to a depth of 3 to 4 feet at a cost of £23. In 1887 a new club house costing about £16 was erected. At the Annual General Meeting on 1st October 1889 'the whole of the office bearers were re-elected with the exception of William Sutherland, who was appointed to the committee in room of Archibald Anderson, deceased'. This is the only reference to this old indefatigable member's death.

On 27th October 1887 there was held in Mr. Arch. Anderson's, Peel Street, the usual meeting after a change of President 'for the purpose of handing over the trophies of the club'. The President invited the committee and a few friends to dinner, seventeen present. John Anderson, Ex-President and Mr. John W. Robinson, President made suitable speeches in the handing over of 18 medals, Bell, and Old Banner, acknowledgements and guarantee being signed by Robert Robinson, J.P., and Marcus Robinson, J.P. A happy evening was spent with song and sentiment contributing to the hilarity of the evening.'

17th January 1888—A formal court was held, when fourteen members were initiated to the R.C.C.C. by 'My Lord' Bailie White.

At the Annual General Meeting 28th September 1888 David Muirhead, Secretary, gave a lengthy report on the previous session, which was reproduced in the press. After referring to the poor curling season, he stated that the new club house was comfortable and commodious, that the greater number of members attending the meetings showed an increased interest in the club, and with other better amenities he ventured to add that 'if the clerk of the weather were a little more in our favour, we have within ourselves the making of one of the best clubs in the West of Scotland'.

Events outwith the club's home affairs were discussed and are briefly recorded. When invitations were received from the Lanarkshire Club to join in their bonspiels with Refrewshire, there was some difference of opinion as to taking part in these. That it was agreed to do so was, one imagines, because as keen curlers, it meant another good game. It certainly was not that they had any particular attachment to the Lanarkshire Province. They consistently maintained their adherence to the Dunbartonshire (Tenth) Province in spite of the Royal Club's Annual always entering the club as in Lanarkshire. At the Annual General Meeting of the Tenth Province on 25th October 1882 Mr. John White (Partick) resigned from the chair and Mr. Allan Kirkwood (East Kilpatrick) elected. Three months later the Province decided to make a presentation to Mr. White 'for his long services to the province'. The club subscribed five guineas. Mr. White had been appointed to the chair, when in 1866 the Province was formed, and also had for many years acted as umpire at the matches.

On 10th January 1887 a match took place between the Club and the Partick Commissioners on the Public Park Pond at Whiteinch. 'This match was arranged at the request of the Magistrates and Commissioners. Handles, stones, etc., were provided by the Partick Club. Two rinks took part. A very enjoyable game was played but, as the rinks were mixed it is not necessary to give particulars'. So runs the minute of the exceptional and noteworthy game, as it took place in the first month of the Jubilee year of Queen Victoria's reign. The Magistrates were presumably feeling they should bring a patriotic atmosphere this early into the burgh, and do so while John Frost obliged. Moreover this Public Park had just been finished, but was not to be formally opened till 2nd July of that year, when the ceremony was performed by Provost Sir Andrew McLean. With the consent of Her Majesty it was named Victoria Park in honour of Her Majesty's Jubilee, and as such has since been known. The recent upheavals at Balshagray Avenue and in the park for the northern approaches to the road tunnel under the Clyde have greatly destroyed the beautiful aspect of that end of the park by the cutting down of many fine trees, and have not only demolished a considerable number of the well built stone residences in the area, but disturbed and displaced many worthy residents in the neighbourhood.   In describing Victoria Park in his 'Glasgow Public Parks', published by John Smith and Sons, Glasgow in 1894, Duncan McLellan, Superintendent of Public Parks (1853-1893) states 'Near to Balshagray Avenue spaces have been let to Partick Clubs at nominal rents for the purpose of lawn tennis and curling.   It is proposed to add about sixteen acres on the north side of the park, and in this way additional recreation ground will be provided'.

In the following year, 1888, the Royal Caledonian Curling Club celebrated its Jubilee.   The most noble The Maruqis of Breadalbane, President, in the chair.   There were 360 members present representing 130 affiliated clubs—Partick was represented by five members—James Watson, James White, Archibald Anderson, Robert Carrick and David Muirhead.   The large four-page menu card with its numerous curling phrases was a work of art.   Dr. John Kerr in his *History of Curling* describes—'on the front was a drawing by John Smart, R.S.A. with the inevitable lean crow perched on a twig and perusing a signboard stuck on an old tree-stump, which read as follows "Tak Notice—Jubilee Dinner, Royal Caledonian Curling Club, Waterloo Hotel, Nov. 28th 1888".'   Since 'song and sentiment' have been mentioned in the club minutes up to this time as concomitants of its social events it is not inconsistent to quote the bits of verse which formed the head and tail of the Toast List at this great curlers' occasion—the celebration of the Jubilee of the Royal Club:

> 'Come, fill the glass and send it round,
> Sae jovial and sae hearty;
> Let mirth, unmixed with care, abound
> Amang ilk curling party.
> Aye may we meet wi' social glee,
> Devoid of strife and snarling—
> Sae send it round, wi' three times three,
> To freedom, love and curling.'

> 'In canty cracks, and sangs, and jokes,
> The night drives on wi' daffing,
> And mony a kittle shot is taken
> While we're the toddy quaffing.

Wi' heavy heart, we're laith to part,
But promise to forgather,
Around the tee, some day, wi' glee,
In cauls, cauld frosty weather.'

Office Bearers

Patrons—Mr. and Mrs. Hugh Kennedy till March 1882. Provost H. Kennedy and Rev. John McColl 1882-1884; ex-Provost H. Kennedy 1884-1890; and Sir Andrew McLean and Mr. Alex. Craig Sellar, ex-M.P. 1888-1890.

Presidents—John Stewart, Archibald Livingston, John Anderson, William Sutherland (2 years), John Anderson (2 years), John W. Robinson (3 years).

Vice-Pres.—Arch. Livingston, George Neilson, William Sutherland, John Henderson (2 years), John R. Scotland, John W. Robinson, Capt. James Watson (3 years).

Representative Members—Ex-Provost John White and John Anderson.

Chaplain—Rev. John McColl (3 years), Rev. D. McEwan Morgan (4 years), Rev. T. M. Lawrie (3 years).

Treasurers—Andrew Brunton, Jas. Meiklejohn (2 years), Jas. Scotland (4 years), William McAllister (3 years).

Secretary—Archibald Anderson (5 years), David Muirhead (5 years).

Members—as at 1st October 1880—Regular members:

John Anderson	John Orr	William Frame
John White	John Maxwell	A. Colquhoun
Archibald Anderson	William White	William Pirrie
J. McGilchrist	Jas. Watson	John Somerville
Thos. Dunlop	John Wallace	John Henderson
John Phillips	T. Brownlee	D. Stevenson
George Neilson	John McArthur	Matthew White
David More	John Stewart	A. Livingston
D. Campbell	Robert Martin	William Sutherland
James White	David Caldwell	Hugh Aitken
Thos. Fletcher	John Galt	J. Anderson, Jun.
R. D. Samuels	William Murdoch	

and 44 occasional members.

Grand Matches

30th December 1880—at Carsbreck, North v. South of the Forth, South win by 230 shots. Partick represented by two rinks—386 rinks took part.

James White   26 shots v. Alexander Robertson, Ballechin   8
William Frame 10 shots v. John Macdonald, Scone and Perth   15

15th December 1882—at Carsbreck—North v. South of the Forth. South win 273 up. 418 rinks. Partick represented by two rinks:

Arch. Anderson   9 shots v. John Smple, South Esk   14
R. Dunn   11 shots v. D. McNiven, Lochaber   12

21st December 1886—at Carsbreck— North v. South of the Forth. South win 425 up. 270 rinks engaged. Partick represented by one rink:

Arch. Anderson 19 shots v. Col. Stirling 14

On same day at Lochwinnoch, Inter-Province Bonspiel, Lanarkshire v. Renfrewshire, for South-west of Scotland Grand Trophy. Four Partick rinks skipped by John Anderson, Jas. White, Wm. Frame and Rich. Dunn. 'Ice in very bad condition, raining long before the game finished.' Partick 37 shots down.

12th January 1881—at Lochwinnoch—Lanarkshire v. Renfrewshire Bonspiel. Four Partick rinks skipped by John Anderson, Jas. White, Wm. Frame and Richard Dunn scored 40 shots v. four Castle Semple rinks—29 shots.

Dunbartonshire Province Bonspiels

11th January 1881 at Loch Ardinning—10 clubs competed, ice splendid. John White (Partick) Umpire, Helensburgh win (third time in succession) 58 shots up Partick second, East Kilpatrick third, Carbeth fourth.

Partick skips:

Arch. Anderson 31 v. Sewell, Duntocher   13
David More   23 v. Paterson, Yoker   11
W. Frame   23 v.   Carbeth   14
Jas. White   17 v. Macdonald, Helensburgh   20

12th December 1882—at L. Ardinning—twelve clubs competed. East Kilpatrick winners with four rinks 14¾ up average; Kilmaronock second four rinks 10¼ up; Luss and Arrochar three rinks 6¼ up; Partick five rinks 4⅕ up. Partick skips John Anderson, Arch. Anderson, Jas. White, Andrew Roy and D. Dunn.

5th February 1886—at Dougalston Loch—ice very rough,

weather good, played twenty-one heads; Helensburgh four rinks winners 7½ up average; Baldernock three rinks 7¼ up; Kilmaronock four rinks 5¾ up; Partick five rinks 2⅖ up.   Partick skips:

Arch. Anderson	39 shots	v.	Sutherland, Allander	9
William Frame	23	,, v.	Carbeth	13
Jas. White	4	,, v.	McAuslan, Helensburgh	38
Richard Dunn	22	,, v.	Armstrong, E. Kilpatrick	15
John Maxwell	14	,, v.	Horn, Yoker	15

30th December 1886—at L. Ardinning.   Ice fairly good—thirteen clubs.   Twenty-one heads.   Cardross three rinks winners—17 up average; Kelvindock second three rinks 6⅔ up; Baldernock third three rinks 4 up; Partick down 'a number of shots'.   Partick skips—John Anderson, Arch. Anderson and Wm. Frame.

30th December 1887—at Lochburnie.   Ice good and weather excellent.   Winners Baldernock three rinks 9 up average; second Helensburgh three rinks 8⅔ up; Cardross third four rinks 7¾ up; Partick three rinks four down.   Partick skips—Arch. Anderson, John Anderson, Wm. Frame.

District Medal and Local Matches

Date	Match D. Medal F. Friendly	No. of Rinks	Result for Partick Win or Loss	Opponents, Place and Remarks
29.12.80	D.	3	L 11 down	Old Monkland, Johnston Loch.
13. 1.81	F.	4	W (104-52)	Govan, Govan new pond.
14. 1.81	F.	3	W (57-53)	Gourock, Partick ice.
20. 1.81	F.	4	L (63-67)	Kirkintilloch, Partick ice.
21. 1.81	F.	4	L (61-83)	Helensburgh, Partick ice.
21. 1.81	F.	3	W (53-52)	Yoker, Partick ice.
25. 1.81	F.	4	W (80-60)	Kilmaronock, on Loch Lomond.
14.12.82	D.	3	W (64-50)	Paisley Boreas, Corsebar pond
29.12.84	D.	3	W (68-54)	Carbeth, L. Ardinning, 21 heads.
29.12.84	D.	3	W (68-54)	Carbeth, L. Ardinning, ice true but wet.
16. 1.85	F.	3	W (69-43)	Willowbank, Willowbank new pond.
24. 1.85	F.	3	W (41-35)	Limekilnburn, their pond, exciting game.
11.12.85	F.	3	W (55-51)	Yoker, Yoker ice, thaw set in, 'dry socks and a good dram finished a somewhat unsatisfactory game'.
9. 1.86	F.	4	W (90-68)	Govan, Partick, ice and weather good. 21 heads.
21. 1.86		3	L (58-69)	Kelvindock, Partick, ice bad, snow bree.
7. 1.87	D.	3	L (20 down)	Hamilton, Morrison L. Cambuslang, ice fair.
13. 1.87	F.	3	W (63-47)	Yoker, Partick, ice fairly good.
14. 1.87	F.	3	L (4 down)	Govan, Govan, ice fair.
29.12.87	F.	3	W (65-54)	Yoker, Yoker, weather excellent, ice good.

In those nineteen matches—Archibald Anderson skipped eighteen, John Anderson fourteen, Wm. Frame ten, James White eight, D. More five, J. Maxwell two, A. Roy and Jas. Watson one each.

Club Games for 'The Bell' Rink Medal, etc.

15th and 22nd January 1881—On Partick pond for coals for the poor of the burgh. Total collection of £8.6/6d. which enabled a distribution of thirty-one carts of coal, 12 cwts. each.

On 10th December 1885—The 'Bell' and Rink Medal Competition was held. Arch. Anderson's rink won from Jas. Anderson's (24-8) and John White's from John Anderson's (25-18). The final tie took place on 4th February, when Arch. Anderson with twenty-nine shots won the 'Bell' and Matt White (for his father indisposed) won the Rink Medal with 10 points.

15th January 1887—The game took place for coals for the poor. 'Ice in splendid condition, and a good turn out of the public.' Thirty households received a cart of coal each, distribution being carried out by Archibald Anderson and James White.

Annual Dinners

Social functions during the earlier half of this period, when Archibald Anderson was still Secretary, were few in number and are not fully reported on in the Minutes. The fact that, with the exception of about six weeks in the beginning of 1881 'Jack Frost' was not much in evidence in these parts, no doubt being kept away by the combined influence of the Gulf Stream and westerly winds, which prevailed over Boreas, God of the North Wind.

1881—A Committee Meeting on 15th February appointed a Sub-Committee to arrange a dinner in the Lesser Burgh Hall on 3rd March. There is no further mention of this function.

1882—A dinner took place in that Hall on 16th March, in the Chair Mr. James White—'a very happy evening ended about 10.30'. Archie's natural humour comes out in a footnote to the Minute— 'The dinner paid its own expenses net with 4d. to the good, and I a-a-drank it—say 4d.'

In the years 1883 to 1887 there is either mention of a Committee Meeting deciding against holding a dinner, or no mention of the matter even being considered.

1888—After over five years' abstention from formal festivities, a dinner was held on 7th April in the Lesser Burgh Hall, and the exuberance of members even extended to the Secretary who gave a very full report of the event. The chair was occupied by the esteemed President Mr. John W. Robinson, who was warmly received by about 70 members and friends present.

Toast List	Proposer	Reply
The Queen and Royal Family	The Chair	
Navy, Army and Reserve Forces	The Chair	Lt. Mackenzie
Provost, Magistrates and Council of Partick	A. H. Ewing	Mr. McCrae
The Royal Caledonian Curling Club	Bailie White	Sir Andrew McLean
Partick Curling Club	Mr. McCrae	The Chair
Kindred Clubs and Friends	Croupier Jas. White	Bailie Marr
Our Patrons	Mr. Donaldson	Sir Andrew McLean
The Ladies	Mr. Matt White	Geo. Buchanan
President, Vice President and Office Bearers	Bailie Thomson	Bailie White

'The dinner was a splendid success.'

1889—The Minute of the dinner in the Lesser Burgh Hall on 11th April contains the full report from the *Govan Press*. The Company of about fifty members and friends was presided over by Mr. John W. Robinson, President of the Club. After the loyal and patriotic toasts, the Partick Curling Club was proposed in complimentary terms by Mr. Marshall of Govan and replied to by the Chairman who said 'he understood there was to be no speech-making, and he was not going to make a speech'. After narrating a few things relative to the Club, he thanked the Company for the enthusiastic way they had received the toast and resumed his seat amid applause. Mr. Arch. Anderson, one of the oldest members of the club present, proposed the Royal Caledonian Curling Club and did it very well. Other toasts followed with music and songs by members of the company.

Archibald Anderson, Member 1850-1889

Turning over the pages of the first volume of Club Minutes and the early pages of the second volume one finds that Archie Anderson was, in his day, a keen, keen curler, an active office bearer, and one of the best skips in the West of Scotland. He was perhaps somewhat overshadowed by his better known Club contemporary John Anderson, who, in addition to being one of the original office-bearers appointed at the inaugural meeting in 1842, at eighty-six years of age outlived Archie by about ten years. Archie was initiated to the club in 1850, was appointed a member of Committee in 1854, and from then till his death in 1889 was seldom absent from the list of office-bearers, including those of Representative Member and President. He was Honorary Secretary for sixteen years (1869-85), and his Minutes evoked from a later President— John H. Lamont, himself a pretty wit—the following succinct note written on a loose sheet of paper inserted in the second Minute book—

'The first minute in this ponderous volume relates the fixing of four skips for a game with the Kilmaronock club on Loch Lomand for the 25th January 1881. The skips were duly elected, but the cat must have washed behind her ears, for the match did not come off. The Secretary at this time and for many previous years was Archie Anderson, who kept what he himself describes as a "Spirit Shop" at 4 Peel Street, in Partick. He appears to have been an excellent secretary with a gift for phonetic spelling and a turn of humour. Some examples may be taken at random—"The Vail of Leven is quite as pithy as Vale". The word business proved a pitfall to Archie. It is variously rendered, but bussness is the favourite form.'

During his almost forty years of membership his name appears as a skip in all matches, provincial bonspiels, and in Grand Matches at Carsbreck, at which the club was represented from 1860 till 1886, including the North v. South of the Clyde Match at Lochwinnoch in 1864 when Partick were highest up club on the losing side. On that occasion with four rinks they were 41 shots up, of which total Archie's rink scored 26 up (27-1).

He was one of the Committee appointed by the Club to negotiate with Mr. Ross the donor of the 'Old Partick Bell' in 1859, and was one of five members who attended the Jubilee dinner of the Royal Club in Edinburgh on 28th November 1888. He was still an active committee member in 1889, and, being 'one of the oldest members of the Club present' remarked the *Govan Press* report of the function, proposed the toast of the 'Royal Caledonian Curling Club' at the annual Club dinner in the Lesser Burgh Hall on 11th April, Mr. John W. Robinson, President, in the chair.

That was his last Club appearance, as the minute of the Annual General Meeting on 1st October that year records that the 'office-bearers and committee of last year were re-elected with William Sutherland added to the Committee in room of Mr. Archibald Anderson, deceased'.

One marvels how Archie got through his secretarial duties during the sixteen years he held the office. Writing obviously was a considerable effort to him, while his phonetic spelling gives one the impression that, even if a dictionary were readily available, he just assumed the readers of his minutes and letters knew what he meant. His descriptions were so clear and brief that readers of his manuscript were in no doubt as to the subject matter. It probably never occurred to him that a century later his efforts would be subject to such close scrutiny.

1890-1900

During this period a most important move was made by the Club —the decision to approach the Commissioners of the Burgh for a lease of ground at the nearly finished new public park at Whiteinch in 1893. The negotiations with the Town Council were satisfactorily completed by a twenty year lease at £7 per annum of ground at the Balshagray Avenue end of the park and alongside ground already leased to the Partick Tennis Club. The Club lost no time in having a pond formed and it was formally opened on 8th January 1894 by Provost Caird of Partick. In the words of the minute 'The President, Captain James Watson, on behalf of the members of the Club, welcomed the Provost and Commissioners, thanked them for their presence and invited the Provost to play the first stone and declare the pond open. The Provost returned thanks for the high honour, spoke a few words of encouragement to the members, and, stepping on to the pond, played the first stone on a very good sheet of ice midst the cheers of a very large and representative gathering, and declared the pond open. Members and friends and representatives from invited clubs including Yoker, Govan, Baldernock, Kelvindock and Campsie Glen formed themselves into rinks and enjoyed some splendid curling. The 'Innerman' was well looked after by the committee appointed for that purpose, who were awarded a hearty vote of thanks for the excellent arrangements they had made. This opening day was the only day's curling of season 1893-94, as a complete thaw set in that night and there was no further frost.

However, that season was followed by a phenomenally hard and a long one—a year spoken of for many years after. Loch Lomond was frozen all over for a long spell; skaters from near and far arrived in their hundreds and were skating without trouble from Balloch to Luss. The pleasure steamers, laid up on shore near Balloch, were opened up as restaurants and did a roaring trade. Partick Club Minutes record matches from January 3rd to February 21st, so the members must have been justifiably satisfied by the timely and successful move of their pond to a more open position in pleasant surroundings.

No doubt as a result of the previous winter's saturnalian festival of curling, *The Badminton Magazine of Sports and Pastimes* in January 1896 produced an article on 'Curling' by E. H. Lawson

Williams. A few short excerpts from it give a contemporary writer's description of that notable year. The article is headed by seven lines from Allan Ramsay (1686-1758):

> 'Sound, sound the music, sound it,
> Let hills and rocks rebound it
> In praise of Scotia's game,
>   Used as a sport it pleases
>   And mind of joy it raises
>   And throws off all diseases—
> How wonderful thy fame!

'The first nine weeks of the year 1895 will ever be memorable as the great ice period of modern times, until, at any rate, if so it chance, some other period of sixty days and more of hard weather exceed it. Not since 1795 had there been such severe and continuous frost. . . . Countless were the Bonspiels played and even the great match between Scotland and England came off, without interruption, near Carlisle.'

The article then has some pages on the game and how it is played, and on the Royal Caledonian Curling Club. The writer then ventures to express his Victorian views on ladies playing the game thus—'More than half of the Scottish clubs have ladies of rank and position as Patronesses—a fact which shows how popular the game is with the fair sex. Some fifty years ago we read of matches played between rinks of young Amazons, and during recent winters, the "New woman" has come forth in all her glory, broom in hand, to throw the channel-stane; but in my opinion she looks better *off* the crampit and should only take part in those games which show off to perfection the grace of her proportions, and the charm of her figure; swinging even a 36 lb. Ailsa is not one of these. Long, however, may the fair ladies of the land look upon the game with favour, and accept the invitations to the annual curlers' balls!

'It is a very fever is curling. The doctor deserts his patients, the minister his flock, the tradesman his counter, and the farmer his herds, all to revel in the glories of the game, and vie with each other in deeds of skill and good-natured badinage.' (The article finishes with these four lines).

> 'Now fill a bumper to the brim,
> And drink wi' three times three, man,
> May curlers on life's slippery rink
> Frae cruel rubs be free, man.'

On 2nd June 1896 the following advertisement appeared in the *Glasgow Herald*:

Glasgow Real Ice—Skating Palace—
Today—The Triumph of the Age

with Curling (Trial) Match from 9.0 to 11.0 a.m., to which all members of Curling Clubs are invited and admitted free on presentation of card.

Skating on the most superb Ice Surface in Europe.   Three Sessions daily— 10.0—12.30 2/-; 2.30—5.30 3/-; 7.0—10.30 2/-; Weekly Tickets 7/6; Spectators' Balcony 1/-.

The Palace Orchestra plays afternoons and evenings.

The Minute Book states—'eight players forming two rinks, took part in a game on this date within the Glasgow Real Ice Co.'s Skating Palace, Sauchiehall Street, Glasgow.   The game lasted two and a half hours and nineteen heads were played and resulted in a win for Mr. White of eight shots.   There was a beautiful sheet of ice, which was very keen, and, although the length of the rink was some yards shorter than usual (thirty yards being the extreme distance' the game was thoroughly enjoyed by players and spectators alike.   This was the first game ever played in Scotland on artificial ice.   The players were afterwards entertained to lunch by the skips (Matthew White, President of Partick C.C., and William McColl).   Mr. White complimented the Partick Club on being the first to play on artificial ice, and predicted a success for the game which had been so successfully inaugurated that day.   The other players were T. W. Shannon, A. Wotherspoon, James T. Ward, David Muirhead, James Craig and George Kirkwood.'

On 29th January 1895—International, England v. Scotland, at Talkin' Tarn, Cumberland.

One rink, Wm. Sutherland skip.

This decade brings us to the end of the nineteenth century, a period of extraordinary progress in the life and habits of our people.   During it the game of curling, which had flourished in the two or more earlier centuries in many parts of Scotland as a winter sport, was brought under a central control by the formation of the Grand Caledonian Curling Club in 1838, which event is dealt with in the introduction.

By its Constitution and Code of Rules, drawn up by a Council of eminent men, who knew the game, and who, in their several clubs and societies, already had experience of bringing the chaos of many codes of rules into order, the Grand Caledonian Club soon proved itself to be and established itself as the efficient supreme head-quarters of the game. This it has so successfully continued to be, that, when the game was later introduced into overseas dominions and foreign countries by emigrant Scots, the Royal Caledonian Curling Club, as it had become by the gracious approval of Her Majesty Queen Victoria in 1843, willingly accepted these loyal and enthusiastic overseas clubs as affiliated members of the Parent Club.

The new century came in with war—the Boer War as an unsettled issue. It started in the autumn of 1899, but so far there is no mention if it in the minutes, though many young volunteers from the Clyde area went to South Africa with detachments of Yeomanry, Infantry and other Corps.

At the Annual General Meeting on 24th October 1899 'a letter from Mr. M. Hunter Kennedy was read, stating that if the club could obtain from the Commissioners the necessary amount of ground to form two artificial rinks, he would find the money to make them'. On the motion of Mr. Lamont seconded by Mr. W. L. Duncan it was unanimously agreed to thank Mr. Kennedy for his generous offer. The Committee were asked to deal with the matter. By 20th February 1900 permission had been granted to construct artificial rinks as per plan submitted. Later the same year, 18th October, Bailie Kennedy presented a plan of a house, which he proposed to erect and present to the Club. At the Annual General Meeting a week later, Mr. McColl, President, moved that a 'hearty vote of thanks be awarded to Messrs. M. H. Kennedy and John Kennedy for the handsome gift of two artificial rinks, and to Bailie Kennedy for his equally generous gift of a new club house'. Mr. M. H. Kennedy and Bailie Kennedy suitably replied and the Secretary was instructed to write the donors as follows—'That the members desire to heartily thank Messrs. M. H. and John Kennedy for the handsome gift they have given to the Club, one which will always be appreciated by the members and prove a source of great pleasure to the players' and 'That the members desire to heartily thank Bailie Kennedy for the handsome club house he has gifted to the Club at this time, a gift which supplies a long-felt want, and confers a boon on the members which will ever be appreciated'.

Excepting the long frost of early 1895, curling during the other seasons of this decade was somewhat spasmodic. There were three grand matches, seven provincial bonspiels and sixteen District

Medal and friendly games with neighbouring clubs; and the Secretary notes some of the many dates when members engaged in games among themselves on the old and new rinks.

From the minutes of these seasons the following items may be mentioned. On 25th December 1890 the President, Mr. John W. Robinson, offered a prize of a pair of curling stones to be played for in rinks, fifteen heads. The winning rink to play down till the winner be declared. The first round was played on 30th December in dull cold weather and on damp ice. Only two rinks turned up, skips John Anderson and Richard Dunn. The latter won 15-7, but there is no record of which member in Dunn's rink won the play-down and the President's prize. The A.G.M. in 1892 records with regret the death of R. Carrick. In 1895 the entry money for new members was raised to 20/- and the subscription was kept at 7/6d. The names of skips appointed for the season was announced and recorded and this continued to be done in following years.

A committee at this time arranged that notice of the condition of the ice at the pond, and notices regarding matches, etc., should be posted on the Messrs. Kirkwood's window; same information to be obtained at Gordons' telephone. The Secretary (Geo. Kirkwood) in his printed and circulated report to the A.G.M. of 1896 recorded 'the loss sustained by the deaths of ex-Provost Kennedy, ex-Provost White and Mr. Sam Dunn, three of its oldest members'. Ex-Provost Kennedy was a very old member, having been initiated so far back as 1849, becoming one of the Club's Patrons in 1877. Ex-Provost White was also a very old and enthusiastic member, initiated in 1849, President in 1850 and representative member in 1855, a position he filled for over twenty-five years.

Mr. More was a popular and genial member whose presence we will sadly miss on the ice. They were all keen curlers and good friends of the Club. In this year it was agreed to limit the membership to one hundred, excluding life members. In 1897 President Matthew White presented twelve new crampits 'of the sort that would stand to be handed down through the heavy mists of antiquity'. Present old members are sure that many of those still in use are of the 1897 vintage and, in the intervening years, have survived many journeys to and from Grand Matches and Province Bonspiels.

The A.G.M. of this year passed the new constitution and rules and ordered those to be printed and circulated among the members.

On 4th November 1898, a Committee meeting under heading 'Refreshments'—'It was agreed that each player pays 1/6d. at home matches. The skips to collect same and hand it to Treasurer'. This minute also gives a list of life members, eleven in number.

In the R.C.C.C. Annual of 1898-99 appeared a special article headed 'A Glasgow Veteran, Mr. John Anderson'—John died on 15th March 1899. The minute book of this time has press cuttings from a local paper and from *The Scottish Referee* of their obituary notices.

Office-bearers—1890-1900

Patrons—J. Parker Smith, Esq. of Jordanhill, M.P., who held office from October 1890 till 1900; Sir Andrew McLean (October 1893-1900); Ex-Provost Kennedy (October 1893-95, when he died); Provost Caird (1896-1900).

Honorary Members—1893—Ex-Provost Kennedy, ex-Provost White, John Anderson, Revd. T. M. Lawrie; and from 1896 Revd. John Smith William Frame.

Honorary President—John W. Robinson from 1893. He had been President since October 1887, wrote notes to the A.G.M.s in 1891 and 1892 resigning his position, when the Secretary was instructed to inform him it had been 'negatived unanimously and the annual meeting had again elected him'. He must have been a genial personality in the chair.

Presidents—John W. Robinson till 1893, Captain Watson (two years), Matthew White (two years), W. H. Kennedy (two years) and W. McColl (1899).

Vice Presidents—Captain James Watson (three years), William Sutherland (two years), William Kennedy (two years), Wm. McColl (two years), M. H. Kennedy (one year).

Representative Members—Bailie White and John Anderson (three years), Provost White and Captain Watson (three years), Capt. Watson and W. Sutherland (four years).

Chaplain—Revd. Thos. M. Lawrie (five years), Revd. John Smith (five years).

Treasurer—W. McAllister (nine years), A. Caldwell (one year).

Secretary—David Muirhead (nine years), Geo. Kirkwood (one year).

List of Regular Members at 1st October 1890

John Anderson	Matthew White	D. Muirhead
John White	John W. Robinson	John Orr
James White	W. Sutherland	John Barton
John Maxwell	Richard Dunn	Geo. Kirkwood
William White	Sam. More	Jas. Kay
James Watson	Hugh Aitken	Thos. Price
William Frame	W. McAllister	John Dawson
J. Henderson	W. F. Bell	R. Carrick

and 31 *occasional members, including—*

Arch. Stewart	William Kennedy	William Kirkwood
H. Kennedy	Marcus Robinson	Matthew White (2)

_____

Grand Royal Club Matches

9th December 1892—At Carsbreck, 150 rinks took part; match ended with a win for South 475 shots up. Partick were represented by two rinks skipped by William Frame and William Sutherland, both down.

8th January 1895—At Carsbreck, 174 rinks engaged, and South won by 273 shots up. Partick was represented by six rinks, who travelled in a special saloon carriage. The minute records the weather was magnificent and the ice keen and clear and gives the skips and their results:

James Watson	13 v. Jas. Isles, Blairgowrie	16
Wm. McColl	12 v. G. G. McLaren, Blairgowrie	14
Wm. Sutherland	15 v. Rev. W. Finlay, Saline	8
R. Lindsay	5 v. Dr. Calberch, Dunkeld	20
Wm. Fulton	7 v. Athol McGregor, Dunkeld	25
Wm. Frame	21 v. George Kean, Saline	7
	—	—
	73	90
	—	—

26th January 1897—At Carsbreck, 247 rinks engaged, result a win for South by 906 shots up. Partick minute records beautiful ice and lovely weather. The Club was represented by three rinks, and their results were:

Jas. T. Ward	15 v. John Douglas, Tullymet	11
W. McColl	13 v. Lt. Col. McLaren, Balquhidder	19
Wm. Kennedy	12 v. Allan Proctor, Balquhidder	16
	40	46

'An exceedingly enjoyable day was spent.'

31st January 1899—At Carsbreck, 226 rinks took part, and South won by 770 shots up. The minute stated the weather was fine, the ice splendid and a thoroughly good game enjoyed. Three rinks represented Partick.

Wm. McColl	10 v. G. G. Gourlay, Broughty	17
James Kay	14 v. J. McDonald, Trossachs	14
A. Wotherspoon	16 v. S. G. Roan, Torry	16
	40	47

9th February 1900—At Carsbreck, 221 rinks engaged in the match which South won by 809 up.

Tenth Province

The Province held its first official dinner in Ferguson and Forresters' Restaurant, Buchanan Street, Glasgow, on 13th January 1893, when 106 members from the affiliated clubs attended. John White (Partick), who had been its first President for twenty-three years, proposed the toast of Tenth Province.

Their second dinner was in the North British Station Hotel on 12th March 1897. J. W. Stewart (East Kilpatrick) occupied the chair, and the croupiers were James White (Partick) and William Stewart (Dalmuir). Apologies for absence were intimated from T. Ripley Ker, Esq., President, and Major McIntyre (Cardross).

The next dinner on 3rd March 1899 was also held in the N.B. Station Hotel, fifty members from the clubs present. J. W. Stewart (East Kilpatrick), President, in the chair.

Province Bonspiels

8th January 1891—On Dougalston Loch. Weather indications of a thaw, snow fell throughout and conditions unfavourable. Carbeth with two rinks won with average of 11 up, and were the first winners of the Kirkwood Cup, presented by the late President Allan Kirkwood.

Partick were second 5⅓ up; Kelvindock third 5 up; Duntocher, Kilmaronock and Helensburgh followed in that order. Other six clubs were down, and Vale of Leven were only absentees. Results of the three Partick rinks:

John Anderson	16	v. Baldernock	10
Wm. Frame	27	v. Helensburgh	16
Richard Dunn	11	v. Kelvindock	12
	54		38

16th January 1892—On Loch Burnie. Weather all that could be desired, ice though a trifle rough was very keen, so a good game was the result. Cardross won with 8½ average up; Vale of Leven second 6¼; E. Kilpatrick third 6 up. Results of three Partick rinks:

Wm. Frame	24	v. Baldernock	15
John Anderson	19	v. Vale of Leven	10
Wm. Sutherland	15	v. Strathblane	25
	58		50

10th December 1892—At Loch Ardinning 'in worst possible weather—rain falling throughout the whole game. Ice dour and wet and rough'. East Kilpatrick winners four rinks 9¼ average up per rink; Yoker three rinks second 9 up; Strathblane three rinks 7⅓ up; Helensburgh four rinks 3¾ up; eight clubs down. All clubs present except Luss and Arrochar.

5th January 1895—On Dougalston Loch. Ice dour, Scotch mist. Baldernock winners 13½ up average per rink; Helensburgh second 7¼; Strathblane third 7; E. Kilpatrick fourth 5 up; Partick 15 down. Partick skips:

Capt. Watson	3 down	v. J. Harvie, Yoker
Wm. Sutherland	12 down	v. W. H. Kidston, Helensburgh
John Anderson	3 up	v. J. Glen, Cardross
Matt White	3 down	v. J. W. Stewart, E. Kilpatrick.

22nd January 1897—On Dougalston Loch. Beautiful ice and strong wind. Duntocher winners 9⅔ up; Helensburgh second 8¾; Partick third 6½ up; four rinks from Partick—skips: Matt White, Jas. Watson, Wm. Sutherland, Wm. McColl.

4th February 1899—On Dougalston Loch. Beautiful weather, lovely ice. Helensburgh won the cup, five rinks 15¼ up average; Kilmaronock second 12 up; E. Kilpatrick third 5 up; Partick four rinks—details:

H. Kennedy	15 v. A. Bulloch, E. Kilpatrick	22
Matt White	17 v. E. Bardsley, Vale of Leven	16
W. McColl	21 v. W. Learmonth, Milngavie	15
W. McAllister	12 v. A. Lindsay, Helensburgh	29
	—	—
	65	82

10th February 1900—On Dougalston Loch. Eleven clubs engaged (Luss and Vale of Leven absent). Snow lay to depth of eight inches, but twenty-one rinks were cleared and 160 players got started soon after noon. Ice excellent and weather of the best.

Baldernock winners four rinks 8¾ up average; second Helensburgh five rinks 6 up; third Cardross four rinks 5¾ up; fourth Strathblane three rinks 4 up; eighth Partick four rinks 7½ down. Partick skips (appointed 6th November 1899): Wm. McColl, Hunter Kennedy, Matt White, William Kennedy and D. Muirhead as reserve.

District Medal and Friendly Games

Date	Match D. Medal F. Friendly	No. of Rinks	Result for Partick Win or Loss	Opponents, Place and Remarks
19. 1.91	D.	2	L (38-44)	Allander, Dougalston L., thaw, ice dour.
28.12.92	D.	3	L (27-88)	Cambuslang, Westburn Green, good day, ice dour.
4. 1.93	F.	5	L (84-92)	Baldernock, Dougalston L., snow, ice keen.
12. 1.93	F.	3	L (41-71)	Yoker, Yoker, magnificent ice, fine weather.
16. 1.93	F.	3 and 1 Jnr.	W (85-69)	Lennox Castle, Lennox, thaw and later frost. Junior rink won match 20 up, others 4 down.
7. 1.95	F.	3	W (70-57)	Yoker, Partick, beautiful day, splendid ice.
25. 1.95	D.	3	L (20 down)	Bothwell, Partick.
28. 1.95	F.	4	W (85-56)	Baldernock, Partick, splendid ice and weather.
6. 2.95	F.	5	L (83-87)	Lilybank, ?, keen game, lovely conditions.
12. 2.95	F.	4	W (81-66)	Kilmaronock, Loch Lomond, good day, ice keen.
18. 2.95	F.	4	L (57-95)	Hamilton, Partick, good weather, keen ice.
21. 2.95	F.	4	L (60-92)	Gourock, Gourock, bright sun, later dour ice.
21. 1.97	D.	3	L (44-56)	Northern, Johnston Lake, ice firm but rough.
30. 1.99	F.	3	W (53-27)	Yoker, Yoker, ice dour and damp.
3. 2.99	F.	4	L (49-71)	Lilybank, Lilybank, fine day, ice splendid.
6. 2.99	D.	4	L (63-93)	E. Kilpatrick, Dougalston, good after snow cleared.

Of these sixteen matches Partick won five and lost eleven.

William Sutherland skipped in nine, Matthew White eight, John Anderson and William Frame seven each, George Kirkwood five and ten other members in three or under three. Evidently the Club was missing its two stalwarts—Archibald Anderson, who died in 1889, and John Anderson, who played in only seven of the above, his last in February 1895 (v. Lilybank).

During these years each player in home matches with other clubs was required to pay 1/6d. to the Treasurer for the refreshment fund.

Club Games

30th December 1890—Play for President John W. Robinson's prize of a pair of curling stones commenced today. Only two rinks turned up on damp ice in dull cold weather. Skips John Anderson and Richard Dunn. Dunn's rink composed of Thos. Price, Wm. Sutherland and Jas. Watson won by 8 shots. There is no record of who won the play down and the President's prize.

8th December 1892—Bell and Rink Medal Competition. In rain and sleet and on poor ice. John Anderson's rink won the Bell over Matthew White (33-24) who got the Rink medal.

11th January 1895—Points game (the first for fifteen years). Good keen ice. John Watson first prize, Matthew White second, T. W. Shannon third, and Wm. McColl fourth.

26th January 1895—Bell and Rink Medal Competition. A large number of members took part. Mr. John Anderson's rink were highest up against Matthew White (25-14) and won the Bell; Mr. Hugh Aitken was next highest up (3 over his opponents) and won the Rink medal.

19th January 1897—Points game, on dour ice. Twenty members entered. First W. McAllister 25, second A. Caldwell 12, third A. Wotherspoon 9, fourth W. Duncan 8.

2nd February 1897—Bell and Rink Medal Competition. Ice fair—two rinks took part. W. Kennedy beat M. White; W. Sutherland won from John Anderson; in final W. Sutherland won the Bell from W. Kennedy, who won the Rink medal.

28th January 1899—Bell and Rink Medal Game. In good weather and on good ice. Three rinks (twenty-four players) played nine heads. H. Kennedy beat W. McColl by 1 shot; M. White from J. Anderson by 9 shots; and Jas. Watson from M. Robinson by 1 shot. In next round M. White beat Jas. Watson by 1 shot, Kennedy a bye. Final H. Kennedy beat M. White by 2 shots and won the Bell. 'This finished one of the best day's curling for this trophy.'

2nd February 1899—Points game in 'beautiful sunny weather, ice dour in consequence'. Result R. Lindsay 20 (President's prize); second W. L. Duncan 18 (Vice President's prize); third A. C. Wallace 16 (W. B. Johnston's prize); fourth W. Kennedy 16 (A. Wotherspoon prize) and fifth H. Kennedy 15 (his own prize).

Games for Coals for the Poor

24th January 1893—The Secretary reported having collected £4.6/0d., with which he and the Treasurer were appointed to distribute the coals.

12th January 1895—In beautiful weather and on first class ice this game was played today by the largest turn-out of members ever seen on the pond, amongst whom was J. Parker Smith, Esq., M.P., who took part in the game. At the finish the Treasurer announced that over £5.10/0d. had been subscribed.

1st February 1897—Annual games played today. A good turn-out of members and good ice. Sum collected £3.19/0d. with which seven tons of coal were distributed.

The Secretary mentions much play by members on the pond, especially in 1892, during the long frost of early 1895, in the winter of 1896-97 and in January 1899.

Dinner and Social Functions

During these years were few. There was an Initiation Court on 3rd March, 1893, Bailie White officiating, when fifteen members were made members of the Royal Club. After the ceremony Captain Watson proposed a vote of thanks to Bailie White, who responded. A few songs ended a happy evening. Other initiating ceremonies are mentioned, but of these there are no minutes.

On 14th January 1895 a Committee meeting unanimously agreed 'that we have a supper this year on 5th February', and appointed a Committee to deal with the matter. There is no further minute so we may assume they were so busy curling during this long frost that there was no time for dining. The A.G.M. on 20th October 1898 agreed that a supper or other social function be arranged, the date to be fixed by the Committee. Again there is no further mention of this taking place. On 21st February 1900 a Committee meeting agreed to have a beef and greens supper on 13th March, the Secretary to send reply postcards to all members asking attendance at the Supper, and subscriptions towards testimonials to the ex-Secretary and to the ex-Treasurer, these testimonials to be presented at the Supper. The price of supper to be 3/0d. On 1st March a Committee meeting arranged the menu and the toast list.

Menu

Curlers' Fare—Hunters Beef and Curley Greens,
Roast Beef and Spuds, Haggis and a free drappie o't.

Toast List

The Queen	The Chair
The Prince and Princess of Wales	The Chair
Army, Navy and Reserve Forces	H. Kennedy
Reply	Captain Watson
Testimonials	Bailie Kennedy
Replies	D. Muirhead, Wm. McAllister
Magistrates and Commissioners	Bailie Fulton
Reply	Provost Hood
Kindred Clubs	Bailie Kennedy
Reply	?

On 10th April—A Committee meeting in Mr. McColl's shop in Kelvin Street. 'Accounts in connection with Testimonials and the Supper were submitted and found correct, there being a surplus of nine pence. The liquid portion of the entertainment (a very considerable item) was generously provided by President McColl gratis, who received a hearty vote of thanks.'

Present members of the Club in this A.D. 1900 will have nostalgic thoughts about the possible cost of 'the liquid' portion of this entertainment, seventy years ago, when whisky was 10 to 15 u.p. at 2/0d. per bottle. Later in 1920 the late Professor George Saintsbury of Edinburgh University wrote 'The Budget has just paid a fresh and flattering if inconvenient compliment to the patriotism of good drinkers'. It is extremely doubtful, were he alive today, if this patriot's comment on the recent Budget of November 1968 would be couched in such moderate language.

A Glasgow Veteran
Mr. John Anderson

Mr. John Anderson, Partick C.C., one of the oldest curlers in Scotland, whose portrait we give, was born in September 1812 at Dumbreck, near Glasgow, and consequently reached the ripe age of eighty-six years in September of this year. Mr. Anderson, better known as 'Long John', is the Father of the Partick C.C. and although his years are long past the allotted span, is a splendid specimen of a man—hale and hearty, and able and willing yet to skip a rink to victory. He stands six feet five inches high and weighs fifteen stones. How few men can boast of such dimensions at his years. Mr. Anderson's curling career started over sixty years ago, the first match in which he took part was when assisting Govan Parish against Eastwood Parish, played on Sir John Pollock's dam in the year 1836, eight players a side, one stone each player. It is, however, when Mr. Anderson assisted at the formation of the Partick Curling Club in 1842 that we have the first documentary evidence of him as a curler. We find from the minutes of the Club that he was appointed one of the Committee at the first meeting, held on 1st April 1842. In the following year (1843) he was elected President, and immediately thereafter was appointed one of the skips of the club. And all down those intervening 55 years we find him skipping in almost every game, Royal, provincial or club.

Skipping for fifty-five years is a record which would be hard to beat. Mr. Anderson's connection with the Partick Curling Club has been of the very closest, as is evidenced by the fact that he has occupied the position of its President ten times (that of Vice President on two occasions) and as representative member to the Royal Club almost uninterruptedly from 1858 to 1892. There is scarcely a minute of a meeting since the Club's inception in 1842 or a list of skips in which Mr. Anderson's name does not figure. Mr. Anderson relates to the writer the most eventful occasion in his curling career. This was when he spent, on one occasion, thirty-six consecutive hours on the ice. He started at six o'clock in the morning with a few friends just to give them a game before they went to business at ten o'clock. When these departed a fresh lot turned out, who occupied the day till well on in the afternoon; and when darkness set in, and the players were about to depart, a contingent turned up from Govan (their pond having been leaking) and with the aid of a plentiful supply of candles, etc., they curled all through the night and all the following day till six at night, 'but,' added Mr. Anderson, 'I was a young man then, being a bit under 60.' He was also an enthusiastic bowler all his life—Mr. Anderson is esteemed and reverenced by the members of the Partick Curling Club and is a well known figure in curling circles in the West of Scotland and is highly respected, his great height and patriarchal appearance making him a man amongst men. He is at present in the best of health and spirits, and regrets that 'Jack Frost' last winter did not allow him to take part in his favourite pastime.

THIS decade, the first of a new century, started while the country was at war with the South African Republics, a state of affairs which continued for another three years, though it did not in general interfere with the life of the average citizen, or indeed with either his work or his outdoor recreations. During the winter of 1899-1900 the Boers overran part of Natal and the country to the west of their republics, notably the towns of Ladysmith, Kimberley and Mafeking. As each of these were in turn relieved, there were great rejoicings, in Partick as elsewhere, when apprentices and other irresponsibles downed tools after the breakfast break and took the remainder of the day "off". As their wages were from 4/0d. to 8/0d. per week of fifty-four hours, these "mafekings" as such exuberant patriotism came to be termed, did not, at less than 1/0d. each, much affect their weekly pay!

The new clubhouse and ponds of the club at Victoria Park were in course of construction and formally opened at the beginning of the season 1900-01. The Secretary, in his report of the previous season to the Annual General Meeting on 2nd October 1901, said:

"The year has seen the Club enriched by the generosity of several members. The new stone house, gifted by Bailie William Kennedy, was ready for use throughout last winter, and those members who took part in the games must have appreciated the boon conferred on the Club by this handsome gift. The ice on the pond afforded very few opportunities for curling, but, thanks to Messrs. M. H. and John G. Kennedy, we had several days' play on the rinks presented by them. No season could have suited better for demonstrating how much we are indebted to these gentlemen."

At this time, so soon after the Club had obtained from the Corporation of the Burgh a long lease of a suitable piece of ground at the north-east corner of the new Victoria Park at Balshagray Avenue, it was very fortunate to have such enthusiastic and keen members as the three Kennedy brothers. In many other ways their practical and influential interest in the game was demonstrated, as appears from now on in the pages of the Club minutes. But their influence extended far beyond the Burgh—M. H. (Hunter) and J. Guthrie (Johnnie) were leading members of the "gallant company of Glasgow Curlers", who resolved in 1905 to have an ice-rink erected at Crossmyloof. In 1907 Hunter was elected a member of the Royal Club, and in 19   he presented a trophy to the Ladies' League, since known as the Hunter Kennedy (Ladies') League Trophy.

Shortly afterwards Mr. James T. Ward presented the tablets on the clubhouse recording the above gifts. The one in the club room above the overmantel reads: "This Clubhouse House was presented to the Partick Curling Club by Provost William Kennedy 1902". The other on the east gable of the clubhouse facing the rink records: "This pond was presented by Mr. M. Hunter Kennedy and by Mr. John G. Kennedy to the Partick Curling Club 1902".

The report of the Secretary also stated that "several other gentlemen have contributed in some way or other to raise the standard of the Club and, without going into details, I may mention in this connection the following. President McColl, Messrs. James Watson, Jas. T. Ward, William McAllister, David Muirhead, Wm. L. Duncan, A. C. Wallace and A. McDougall and D. D. Gow".

The following season was a long hard one, when there was curling on the rinks from 11th November. This, the minute remarks, is worthy of note as the earliest date on which we, as a club, have had curling. They were curling again on 22nd November, on ten days during December including the "Bell" Competition on the 20th, and ten days during January between the 6th and 25th. There is not much mention of curling in the later seasons of this period, but there must have been some. A Grand Match at Carsbreck took place on 16th January 1903, and a Provincial Bonspiel the same season; and there were a few locals' matches in season 1906-07. A minute does mention "no matches during season 1905-06, but plenty of games on small pond".

The minute of 29th January 1901 states "Frost again, ice good. Today President McColl handed to Messrs. M. H. and J. G. Kennedy small curling stones, suitably mounted and inscribed, for their ladies, as mementoes of the gift handed over by their husbands to the Club". On 20th February, after an Initiation Ceremony conducted by Captain Watson, the Club held a successful social evening, when the President took the chair. During the evening he presented to Bailie William Kennedy a silver biscuit box in the form of a curling stone as a token of his personal appreciation of the Bailie's kindness in erecting such a beautiful clubhouse. The Bailie suitably replied.

In January 1901 the Provost, Magistrates and Councillors of the

Burgh graciously accepted Honorary Membership of the Club to which they had been invited.

At the Annual General Meeting in October 1901 the question of the custody of the "Bell" was raised and remitted to the Committee to go into the matter and report. This they did and passed a resolution on 20th December 1901, later adopted.

Custody of the "Bell"—Resolution passed 20th December 1901

"On account of the growth of the Burgh and of the fact that a great number of the present members reside outside the Burgh boundaries, the Committee think the time has arrived for bringing the terms of Mr. Ross' letter of gift dated 29th April 1859, up to date. They are of the opinion that Mr. Ross meant that his trophy should at no time leave the Burgh excepting eastward into Glasgow, and they consider that they are only respecting Mr. Ross' wishes in now declaring that the Bell cannot at any time be taken beyond the Burgh boundary excepting eastward as already mentioned, but in order that interest may be maintained and that competing rinks may play at their best strength, the winning skip (if he should reside outside the Burgh boundary) shall have the privilege of handing the Bell into the custody of any player in his rink who does reside in the Burgh, provided always that he and his sureties are acceptable to the Directors. In the event of no player in the winning rink being eligible to take custody according to the conditions of this minute, it shall be retained by the President until such time as it has been won from this rink."

The Scottish Ice Rink

The Royal Club Annual of 1906-07 remarked "Ice Rink in Glasgow. A gallant company of Glasgow Curlers met and resolved to have an Ice Rink constructed in the Western Metropolis. It is now being erected. Matches and tournaments could be arranged without any risk of interference from King Thaw, and King Frost would be taught a lesson that would perhaps make him mend his manners". The Annual of the following year under heading—

Inauguration of the Scottish Ice Rink

The rink to which reference was made in last year's Annual is now *un fait accompli*. It was opened with great *eclat* on October 1st in presence of a noteworthy gathering of Knights and Dames. This institution can best be described in French. The writer's break-out into French is in keeping with the national feeling or cult of the time. Fostered by King Edward VII, who was a great favourite in France, the *entente cordiale* did much to smooth down the feathers of the French chanticleer, which had been considerably ruffled by the Fashoda incident in 1898. It may be said to have earned for the King the sobriquet of the "Peacemaker".

"*C'est magnifique*, and, to carry on our foreign vocabulary, there is no doubt that it will have a wonderful influence in promoting *l'entente cordiale* between curlers at home and abroad. Though the enterprise is largely that of a Glasgow company, the patronage of the foremost curlers of the world, represented by the presence of the office-bearers of the mother, the Royal Club suggested a much more national affair. Among others present was the Secretary of the R.C.C.C. Mr. Davidson Smith, whose winter days and nights are supposed to be spent communing with the weather authorities upon the ticklish question of the 'playableness' of Carsbreck. In the unavoidable absence of Lord Strathcona, Sir Charles Dundas, himself an enthusiastic Perthshire curler, performed the opening ceremony. In the afternoon an opening friendly game was played between the Eastern and Western divisions." Twelve rinks a side, result Eastern 116 shots, Western 112; majority for Eastern 4 shots. Captain Watson (Partick) represented and skipped the Tenth Province Dumbartonshire rink and Marcus Robinson (Partick) the Ice Rink Company rink.

Office-Bearers

Patrons—Ex Provost Caird, J. Parker Smith, Esq., of Jordanhill, M.P., and Sir Andrew McLean; and from 1909 Sir A. Kay Muir, Bart.

Honorary Members from 1901—The Provost, Magistrates and Councillors of Partick with the Rev. J. Smith from 1902 and Captain Cameron from 1904 and William Frame.

Presidents 1900-02—William McColl; M. Hunter Kennedy 1902-10.

Vice-Presidents 1900-02—M. H. Kennedy; 1902-10 James T. Ward.

Representative Members 1900-02—Captain Watson and Wm. Sutherland; 1902-10 Captain Watson and Wm. McColl.

Chaplain 1900-10—Rev. John Smith, D.D.

Treasurer 1900-02—A. Caldwell; 1902-10 John M. Lamont.

Secretary 1900-10—William Ward.

Regular Members in October 1900

James Watson	James Kay	William Ward
Matthew White	Thos. Price	Matthew White (2)
Wm. Sutherland	William McColl	A. Caldwell
Hugh Aitken	W. L. Duncan	M. H. Kennedy
Wm. McAllister	James T. Ward	J. Fulton
Joseph Muir	William Kennedy	A. Wotherspoon
John M. Lamont	R. Lindsay	H. Fulton
D. Muirhead	John C. Kennedy	Geo. Kirkwood

and forty-four *occasional members*, including Wm. White, M. Robinson, Wm. Kirkwood, J. W. Robinson, Jas. Gardener, Geo. Smellie, Chas. Connell, J. McIntosh, W. Robinson.

The minutes in 1902 make suitable references to the deaths of Wm. Sutherland and Wm. McAllister, both of whom had been in office for some years, and in 1904 to that of G. H. G. Buchanan.

Grand Matches

11th February 1902—At Carsbreck—North v. South of Forth and Clyde Canal. Two hundred and forty rinks engaged in glorious weather. South won by 638 shots. Partick rinks:

William McColl	10 v. P. McPherson, Lawers & Comrie	23
Jas. T. Ward	25 v. Wm. Wilson, Trinity Gask	9
M. H. Kennedy	16 v. Peter Wilson, Trinity Gask	14
William Kennedy	20 v. John Howe, Kilmarnock	13
James Kay	13 v. Jas. Galbraith, Kilmarnock	12
	—	—
	84	71
	—	—

16th January 1903—At Carsbreck. North v. South of Forth and Clyde Canal. Two hundred and eighty-six rinks engaged. South won by 894 shots. Partick rinks:

William McColl	10 v. Robert Mather, Alva	14
M. H. Kennedy	18 v. Hugh McDermot, Alva	20
Jas. T. Ward	11 v. Atherton Gray, Alva	18
William Kennedy	8 v. John Fleming (Dollar & Devonvale)	16
James Kay	16 v. John S. Henderson (Dollar and Devonvale)	6
	—	—
	63	74
	—	—

April 6-29th 1908—In Scottish Ice Rink. Two hundred and nineteen rinks engaged. South win by 400 shots up. Partick rinks:

M. H. Kennedy 23 v. Robert Scott, Bonhill 13
Jas. T. Ward   23 v. D. Howie, Bonhill   11

46   24

March/April 1909—In Scottish Ice Rink. Two hundred and nine rinks engaged. Majority for South 547. Partick rinks:

M. H. Kennedy 19 v. Major Archibald, Tillycoultry 11
Jas. T. Ward   16 v. Andrew Rodger, Tillycoultry   17
Jas. Kay   10 v. Graham Paton, Tillycoultry   17
William McColl 16 v. Geo. McAlpine, Loch Ard   12

61   57

24th November 1909—At Carsbreck. North v. South of Forty. Three hundred and eighteen rinks engaged. South win by 948 shots. Partick rinks:

William McColl 7 v. Adam Steel, Scone & Perth   19
M. H. Kennedy 14 v. G. Cousin, Alloa   22
Jas. T. Ward   17 v. J. R. Taylor, Tannadice & Oathlaw   20

38   61

Province Bonspiels

13th February 1902—At Dougalston Loch—twenty-five rinks. Two hundred players.

Winners Luss and Arrochar (3 rinks)—7 up average per rink
Second Baldernock   (3 rinks)—6⅓ ,,   ,,   ,, ,,
Third   East Kilpatrick (4 rinks)—6   ,,   ,,   ,, ,,
Fourth Helensburgh   (6 rinks)—5½ ,,   ,,   ,, ,,

Partick (four rinks, skipped by Wm. McColl, Jas. T. Ward, Jas. Kay and M. H. Kennedy) were down 11 shots (64-75).

Fourteen clubs were represented. The ice was in good condition and enjoyable games were had by all.

17th January 1903—On Dougalston Loch. Fourteen clubs took part in the Bonspiel. Ice in capital condition.

Winners Baldernock (4 rinks)—13½ shots up per rink
Second Helensburgh (6 rinks)— 9   „ „   „ „
Third   Partick   (4 rinks)— 7½   „ „   „ „
Partick skips: Wm. McColl, Jas. T. Ward, M. H. Kennedy,
Jas. Kay.

District Medal and Friendly Matches

Date	Opponents	M—Match F—Friendly	Rinks	Partick result W—shots up L—shots down	Remarks
13. 2.01	Yoker	F	2	W (51-33)	At Partick, first match on new pond.
27.12.01	Baldernock	F	5	L (68-111)	At Dougalston Loch.
14. 1.02	Yoker	F	3	W (66-30)	At Partick.
31. 1.02	Hamilton	M	3	L (38-77)	At Hamilton.
31.12.06	Lilybank	F	4	W (34-26)	At Partick, thaw, ten heads only
1.07	Baldernock	F	3	L (23-29)	At Milngavie, thaw, nine heads only.
21. 2.07	Cawder Ho.	M	3	W (64-42)	At Holytown, ice good (R.C. Annual 1910-11).

Club Competitions

On 20th November 1900 it was intended to open the new rinks today, but unfortunately the frost, which had been very keen, disappeared early and it was thought advisable to postpone the event. However, a few members did turn up and it was decided to make the most of what ice was left. The following members were formed into President and Vice-President rinks: President, Wm. McColl (skip), W. L. Duncan, Wm. Ward, A. Caldwell; Vice-President, M. H. Kennedy (skip), J. T. Ward, A. C. Wallace, A. N. Other. The Vice-President's rink won by 5 shots to 3.

7th February 1901—Game for War Fund. A challenge was issued from Bailie Kennedy to Mr. M. H. Kennedy to play a rink game for £5. The ice was in fine condition and the following eight players had a most enjoyable game:

A. Wotherspoon, Wm. Ward, Wm. Kennedy and Wm. McColl (skip) v. Wm. Duncan, J. G. Kennedy, J. T. Ward and M. H. Kennedy (skip).

Result—Wm. McColl 23 shots; M. H. Kennedy 14.

£3.4/0d. was collected on the bank, so that the sum of £8.4/0d. was sent to the fund.

15th February 1901—Points game. The ice weakened as the game went on. With three tests still to go, the game was abandoned and the prize winners received their awards: first W. P. Weir (23);

D

second R. Lindsay (15 points); third Jas. Fulton (13 points) and sixteen others took part in the competition. The winner, W. P. Weir, went out to finish all the tests and succeeded in bringing his score up to 30, a very fine performance considering the wretched state of the ice.

14th February 1901—"Old Bell" Competition.

First round	Wm. McColl's rink	15 v. M. H. Kennedy	5
	T. Price	13 v. W. Sutherland	5
Second round	Wm. Kennedy	9 v. Wm. McColl	7
	R. Lindsay	10 v. T. Price	7
Final	R. Lindsay	10 v. Wm. Kennedy	2

20th December 1901—"Bell Competition". First prize £2.2/0d. presented by Marcus Robinson; second prize £1.1/0d. by Wm. McColl.

Wm. McColl's rink 16 v. M. H. Kennedy 11
Wm. Kennedy   17 v. A. Caldwell   4
Final Mr. McColl's rink 7 v. Wm. Kennedy 5

15th January 1903—"Bell" Competition.

W. P. Weir beat A. C. Wallace by 3 shots.
W. A. Kirkwood beat J. G. Kennedy by 1 shot.
J. T. Ward beat A. Caldwell by 3 shots.

Second round	W. P. Weir, W. A. Kirkwood 8 shots
	(J. T. Ward and bye).
Final	Jas. T. Ward, W. P. Weir, 1 shot.

Social Events

20th February 1901—An Initiation Ceremony was held in Mr. J. N. Boag's, Captain Jas. Watson officiating with the assistance of other ten members. The following were duly admitted to the Brotherhood:

M. Robinson	D. D. Gow	A. Caldwell
A. C. Wallace	Wm. Brown	Jas. Frame
W. L. Duncan	W. A. Kirkwood	Wm. Ward
Wm. Kennedy	A. McDougall	Hugh Fulton
Wm. Fulton	M. H. Kennedy	R. McInnes
Jas. Fulton		

17th March 1902—A Committee of this date records arrangements made for a supper. Fifty tickets had been sold, draft menu approved, toasts arranged, and other details left to sub-committee. (There is no mention at all of the function.)

18th December 1903—An initiation ceremony was held in the Police Gymnasium. Captain Watson presided, and there was a large muster of members. The following were admitted to the Brotherhood:

Robert Robinson	R. Paul	T. G. Kirkham
D. Robinson	P. M. Martin	H. Cowley
W. Robinson	G. E. Raeburn	H. J. McIntosh
Wm. Sorley	Robert Duncan	S. Mechan
J. M. Lamont		

During this period the Tenth Dunbartonshire Province held two dinners in the North British Station Hotel on 12th March 1902 and 25th February 1903. Both were well attended and presided over by the President, J. W. Stewart (East Kilpatrick), who presented the Province Trophies to the winning clubs. On the latter occasion he remarked that since 1860, when the Province was formed, twenty-five bonspiels had been held, eight at Lochburnie, eight at Loch Ardinning and nine at Dougalston Loch; six were played between 1860 and 1870, five from 1870-80, five from 1880-90, six from 1890-1900 and three since. Within that period eleven matches took place in January, six in February, and eight in December—the earliest on 4th December and the latest on 13th February.

Some Don'ts for Curlers

The compilers of the Royal Club Annual for season 1908-09 evidently considered it was time to draw the attention of curlers to the Rules of the Game. To stress their points, they adopted the negative method of emphasising in no uncertain language the things players should not do. As one not infrequently, to use another negative, sees players, especially when sweeping, assuming they know better than their skip, it is perhaps not out of time and place to reproduce them here.

"Don't forget to clean your stone before each shot.

Don't throw the stone; lay the sole on the ice.

Don't delay the game; be ready to play the moment your turn arrives.

Don't skip from the crampit. The person in charge of the house will attend to the skipping, and soopers should obey nobody else.

Don't argue with your skip. He may be, and probably is, an

escaped idiot, who knows much less about the game than you do. Still, he is your skip and as such must be obeyed.

Don't try shots that have not been called for; the skip can judge far better what is wanted than you can possibly do from the crampit, and strict obedience to orders is the first essential of a curler.

Don't be unduly elated at a fluke. Your opponent will probably follow with a worse one.

Don't stand watching the stones go by you; be with them and be ready to 'soop' the moment you are told to do so.''

THIS decade is best remembered, especially by the older members of the Club, as containing the years of the 1914-18 war. The minutes of this period have frequent references to causes of changes in the normal life of the citizens and to the effect of these disturbances on the Club, its members, and their families.

But, before that, in 1912, Partick as a Burgh was absorbed along with Govan and other neighbouring areas by the City of Glasgow Extension Bill. In spite of strong local opposition to that Government sponsored measure, Parliament passed it and the Burgh of Partick came to an end.

The war, following so soon after, seemed, by its immediate mobilisation of all Reserve, Volunteer and Territorial forces, its demands for more men for the Services, its urgent nation-wide requisitioning of all kinds of materials from ships and guns, shells and small arms ammunition, down to needles and thread and seemed to reduce the local City of Glasgow "take-over" of its neighbouring Burghs to a very ordinary amalgamation of interests. Partick and Govan, being highly important national shipbuilding and engineering centres, were immediately and wholly involved. It is, however, noteworthy that several local institutions and clubs continued to carry on their pursuits as providers of healthy exercise for the citizens during their greatly curtailed hours of leisure.

Our own Club rink was in use as often as "Jack Frost" remembered the curlers, and the Crossmyloof Ice Rink was for a time open for skaters and curlers, mainly by the efforts of a Partick Curling Club member.

During the summer of 1911 the City held a very large and, compared to more recent standards, successful Industrial Exhibition in Kelvingrove park, adjoining and just outwith the old Partick Burgh boundary. A Club minute of October in that year includes a cutting from the *Evening Citizen*, "Partick Curling Club at the Annual Meeting held in the clubhouse it was decided to play a match for the custody of the Club trophy, the Old Partick Town Bell at Crossmyloof Ice Rink at an early date. This Bell, which is in a fine state of preservation and handsomely mounted, is one of the objects of interest now on view in the Palace of History at the Exhibition". The Honorary Secretary evidently turned a "blind eye" to the fact of the bell being, during the six months' run of the Exhibition, outside the limits prescribed by Mr. Ross in his Deed of Gift to the Club.

Early in 1911, the President called a special meeting in the clubhouse in response to a request signed by a large number of members. The requisition was to the effect that the constitution and rules were not up to date. A sub-committee consisting of the President, Vice-President and Messrs. Lamont, White and Watson was appointed to draw up a new constitution and rules. On 22nd September a special meeting considered and approved these, and instructed the Treasurer to have them printed and distributed to the members. A copy of the "Deed of Gift" relating to the "Bell" was to be printed at the end of the booklet containing the rules. A copy of the rules as printed is pasted in the minute book.

On 17th November 1911, after an Initiation Ceremony held by the Club, ex-Deacon-Convener White handed to the President on behalf of the Club a "Parchment" that belonged to his father, Provost White, a former President of the Club. President Ward suitably acknowledged the gift and handed it over to the custody of the Secretary. This Parchment bears a printed cypher containing an oath or promise to be made by curlers on their initiation. It is of considerable antiquity.

A cutting from the *Evening Citizen* of Saturday, 25th November 1911, under "Public Notices" reads—"Partick Curling Club— Pond and Electrically-lit Shallow Rinks, applications for Membership may be made to J. M. Lamont, Hon. Sec., 16 Marlborough Avenue". This was authorised to be inserted once weekly for four weeks.

At the Annual General Meeting on 4th October 1912 John G. Kennedy was appointed President. He noted the fact of its being the last year of the existence of Partick as a Burgh, of which his father had been Provost, as well as his eldest brother. Considerable discussion took place as to the effect of annexation of Partick to Glasgow in view of the conditions in the deed of gift of the "Bell". It was resolved to postpone the matter until next Annual General Meeting, by which time annexation will be an accomplished fact. The Annual General Meeting of 3rd October 1913 resumed consideration of the altered circumstances, and on the motion of Mr. John A. Warren, C.E., seconded by Mr. William Ward, the matter was remitted to the office-bearers to frame a resolution supplementary to the resolution minuted on 20th December 1901.

On the 6th October 1913 the *Glasgow Herald* published a paragraph "In annexing Partick, it appears the Glasgow Corporation inherit the possible reversion of the Old Partick Village Bell, a very fine antique specimen, used up till 1779 for announcing births, marriages and deaths, and other events of interest to the community. This bell, belonging to a Mr. John Ross, was presented by him to the Partick Curling Club in 1859, with the proviso that in the event of the membership of the Club in any year falling below the number of eight persons, the bell should become the property of the Magistrates and Commissioners of the Burgh of Partick. But, at the Annual Meeting of the Curling Club, held on Friday, evening, the membership was stated to be upwards of eighty, so the Corporation's campanular reversion seems fairly remote".

This manifesto from the City's leading newspaper evidently did not smooth down the hackles on the Partick Curlers' bonnets since, at a meeting in the clubhouse, Victoria Park, on 18th December (present—Vice-President D. Muirhead, R. J. Borthwick, Robert Robinson, Robert Duncan, R. A. Smellie, David Robinson and J. M. Lamont), the annexed resolution was adopted, and the Secretary instructed to convey to Mr. Warren the thanks of the Committee for furnishing the plan of Partick boundaries on linen, attached to the minute and inscribed "Partick Curling Club Plan, relative to Minute of 20th December 1901 showing limits within which the Partick Old Bell must remain in terms of the deed of gift".

Resolution on Custody of the Old Partick Village Bell presented to the Partick Curling Club by Mr. John Ross (deceased) in terms of his letter of gift, dated Sandyford, Glasgow, 29th April 1859.

———————

In terms of a remit from the Annual General Meeting held on 3rd October 1913 the Office-bearers and Committee of the Partick Curling Club at a meeting duly called hereby resolve that notwithstanding the annexation of the Burgh of Partick by the City of Glasgow as at November 1912, the limits outwith which the above-named Trophy may not be taken as defined in resolution minuted on 20th December 1901 shall be the boundaries of the Burgh of Partick as they existed prior to said annexation and eastward thereof as far as what was formerly 215 Dumbarton Road, Sandyford, Glasgow, all as shown on plan annexed hereto, prepared by

Mr. John C. Warren, Civil Engineer, Glasgow, signed by—
    D. Muirhead   Vice-President (Chairman)
    J. M. Lamont   Hon. Secretary.
    David Robinson   Hon. Treasurer
    R. A. Smellie   ⎫
    Robt. J. Borthwick   ⎬ Members of Committee
    Robt. Duncan   ⎭

19th October 1915—"At a Committee meeting, David Muirhead, President in the Chair, the Secretary reported that Mr. S. Mechan had offered to remount the Bell in a setting which he would submit for approval, but after full discussion it was the opinion of the meeting that, while highly appreciating the kindness and generosity of Mr. Mechan in making the proposal, the Bell had become so identified with the present setting, which had besides itself acquired a certain historical interest, that no change should be made."

Mr. Mechan presented to the Club a Roll of Honour which he had designed and executed and for which he was warmly thanked.

During the war Annual General Meetings were of a purely routine nature but it was minuted that all members serving with the Forces were relieved of their subscriptions.

Office Bearers

Patrons—Ex-Provost Caird, ex-Provost Wood, Rt. Hon. J. Parker Smith, P.C., of Jordanhill, Sir Robert Balfour, Bart., M.P.

Honorary Members—From 1910-12, the Provost, Magistrates and Councillors of the Burgh, ex-Provost William Kennedy, Mr. Chas. B. Connell; from 1913, James Whitton (Superintendent of Glasgow Parks) and James Donaldson (late Town Clerk of Partick).

Presidents—1910-12 Jas. T. Ward, 1912-14 John G. Kennedy, 1914-19 David Muirhead, 1919-20 Robert Robinson.

Vice-Presidents—1910-12 John G. Kennedy, 1912-14 David Muirhead, 1914-19 Robert Robinson, 1919-20 John M. Lamont.

Representative Members—1910-20 W. E. McColl and James Watson.

Chaplain—1910-20 Rev. Dr. Smith of Partick Parish Church.

Treasurers—1910-19 David Robinson, 1919-20 H. J. McIntosh.

Hon. Secretaries—1910-19 John M. Lamont, 1919-20 R. A. Smellie.

Match Secretaries—1910-12 D. Muirhead, 1912-19 ex-President Jas. T. Ward, 1919-20 James Craig.

Regular Members as at September 1910:

James Watson	W. Kirkwood	M. H. Kennedy
Matthew White	A. Caldwell	A. McAllister
W. P. Weir	Thos. Price	David Robinson
D. D. Gow	J. T. Ward	Wilson Robinson
R. Duncan	Wm. Kennedy	Robt. Robinson
Wm. McColl	R. Lindsay	R. J. Borthwick
J. M. Lamont	John Kennedy	Jas. Stewart
D. Muirhead	W. Ward	R. A. Smellie

Occasional Members—Thirty-two including Sam Mechan, Marcus Robinson, Wm. S. Wylie, Chas. Connell, Jas. Stirrat, Robert Paul, Alex. Craig, John A. Warren, Matthew White Jun., W. L. Duncan, Jas. Gardener, J. L. Bennett and Arch. Stewart.

Grand Matches

2nd February 1912—At Carsbreck. Two hundred and eighteen rinks engaged. South won by 439 shots. Partick represented by one rink, G. W. Duckett, David Robinson, W. R. Calder and J. M. Lamont (skip) and were 6 shots up (14-8) against their opponents Largo (skip G. A. Bell). A curious sequel to this Grand Match of 2nd February 1912 came up at a Committee Meeting on 8th March a month later.

"*Claim by Largo Curling Club*—Correspondence was read regarding a claim by the Largo Club for £1.1/0d. in respect of Partick No. 1 rink (W. McColl) having failed to meet them in the Grand Match or notify them beforehand. It was explained that Mr. McColl was in Switzerland when the Grand Match was played, and that owing to a misprint in the official draw 'Largs' was notified instead of Largo. The Secretary was instructed to take the matter up with the Secretary of the Royal Club."

Grand Match at Edinburgh Ice Rink, February to April 1913— Two hundred and twenty rinks engaged. South up 1118 shots. Partick represented by two rinks drawn against Thornton for North.

Partick No. 1

J. G. Kennedy (skip)
W. H. Kennedy, third
Robt. Duncan, second
R. A. Smellie, lead

} 22 shots v. R. Fraser, Thornton 10

Partick No. 2

I. M. Lamont (skip)
D. Muirhead, third   18 shots v. Geo. A. Gibb, Thornton
Robt. Robinson, second   3
H. J. Craig, lead

5th March 1914—At Haymarket and Crossmyloof Ice Rinks. Two hundred and thirty-seven rinks engaged. Majority for South 1046. R.C.C. Annual 1914-15 report Partick represented by three rinks.

J. M. Lamont   8 v. J. Macdonald, Callander   19
D. Robinson   17 v. W. McFarlane, Callander   27
J. G. Kennedy 34 v. A. McFarlane, Carsbreck   6

       —   —
       59   52
       —   —

4th October 1912—At Annual General Meeting "occasion was taken to heartily congratulate the President J. G. Kennedy (skip) and James Stirrat (third man) on having that day won the Kandersteg Reunion Cup at Crossmyloof on a knock-out Tournament in which their rink defeated some of the strongest curling talent in Scotland". A news cutting gives details of the close final (18-17) for Kennedy, the runners up being Cambusnethan (Wm. Lindsay (skip)).

R.C.C. Rink Championship—Season 1912-13

Partick rink—J. G. Kennedy (skip), Wm. McColl, Jas T. Ward and Wm. Ward.

First round   20 shots v. Col. Robertson-Aikman   7 shots
Second round 21   ,,   v. Sixteen Club   9   ,,
Third round   23   ,,   v. Dalry   17   ,,
Fourth round 16   ,,   v. Bridge of Weir   8   ,,

Semi-final beaten by Edinburgh Ice Rink. Partick minute records no account of that match reached the Secretary except the (very good) *Record and Mail* photograph on preceding page.

Waldie-Griffith Inter-Province Match at Crossmyloof, 13th February 1912.

Partick No. 1—J. M. Lamont (skip), D. Robinson, R. A. Smellie and H. J. Craig down 14-18 v. Wigtown.

Partick No. 2—D. Muirhead (skip), W. P. Weir, **D. D.** Gow, A. McAllister won by 1 shot v. Mochram.

Waldie-Griffith Inter-Province Cup, January 1913, at Crossmyloof. Tenth Province v. Lanarkshire Province. Partick rinks, three.

1. J. G. Kennedy (skip)
   M. H. Kennedy
   J. Stirrat
   Thos. Duncan
   } 18 v. Douglas No. 1 (W. Paterson) 15

2. D. Muirhead (skip)
   R. Duncan
   R. Smellie
   Jas. Maitland
   } 12 v. Douglas No. 2 (J. Willison) 14

3. J. M. Lamont (skip)
   D. Robinson
   H. J. McIntosh
   R. J. Borthwick
   } 17 v. Hamilton (Col. Robertson Aikman) 14

Lanarkshire won by 112 to 71 shots.

During this period members of the Club took part in curling further afield and the President, James T. Ward, and Vice-President, J. G. Kennedy, were members of the Royal Caledonian Curling Club team which toured Canada in 1912. Hunter Kennedy, a brother of the latter, played in the international match against England in 1920 and skipped a rink which won 20 shots to 4 against W. Kerr of Preston. A District Medal match against Huntershill was delayed because the tram cars conveying the players were held up by a heavy fall of snow, but Partick lost by 8 shots.

List of Trophies, the Property of the Club,
6th October 1913

Mahogany casket containing silver medals as follows:
R.C.C. District Medal

won 10th February 1864, from Whitevale Club.
4th January 1867, from Lochwinnoch Club.
12th January 1867, from Boreas Club.
27th December 1869, from Kelvindock Club.
28th December 1870, from Bridgeton Club.

Three District Medals, undated-

    won 16th December 1874, from Whitevale Club.

      21st December 1874, from Uddingston Club.

      22nd February 1907, from Cawder House Club.

Four Province Medals, undated

R.C.C.C. 10th Province Medal

    won 14th January 1867, thirteen clubs competed.

      24th December 1874, ten clubs competed.

Medal inscribed "Partick Curling Club, instituted 1842, admitted into the Royal Club 1849".

Medal inscribed "Lanarkshire Curling Club".

Medal (in case) presented to Club for competition by John Wallace.

Medal (in case), third prize 10th Province Bonspiel, 17th January 1903.

    Twenty-one medals in all.

One Silk Banner in japanned case.

The Old Partick Village Bell dated 1726, gift from Mr. John Ross, 29th April 1859.

Curlers' Oath printed puzzle on part of a flour sack, formerly the property of ex-Provost John White, Partick, presented by his son ex-Deacon Convener (of Glasgow Trades House), Matthew White.

(Sgd.) J. M. Lamont,

Hon. Sec., 6th October 1913.

Curling at Crossmyloof Ice Rink, 1916-17,
from the R.C.C.C. Annual, 1917-18

Owing to the falling off in attendance in 1915-16 due to the war, the Directors of the Scottish Ice Rink Company decided last autumn reluctantly not to open the rink for season 1916-17. That popular and keen curler, Mr. Hunter Kennedy, however, came to the rescue, and, being Chairman of the Ice Rink Curling Club, succeeded in raising a Guarantee Fund of £2,000 and getting his club to take over the rink for the time being, paying a certain rental and keeping it open so that curlers in and around Glasgow should not quite be deprived of their pet recreation. This venture was so far successful, the Guarantors having to meet only a trifling loss, while they had the gratification of seeing the brethren having a good time.

To his many friends in the West, and generally in the Royal Club, of which he was for a time one of the Members of Council, it was particularly gratifying that Mr. Hunter Kennedy, to whose enterprise and enthusiasm the continuance of last season at Crossmyloof was mainly due, figured so prominently in the prize list. It is also very pleasing to hear from the Secretary, Mr. James Gourlay, that out of a total amount of prize money of between £60 and £70, more than two-thirds of that sum was handed back to him to be forwarded to the Scottish Branch of the British Red Cross Society.

The Royal Club Annual of 1919-20 records that during the season 1917-18 the Scottish Ice Rink "was in the unique position of being the only ice rink in the U.K. open for curling and skating". Shortly after the season ended in March the Crossmyloof rink was purchased outright by William Beardmore for the making of aero engines, and will not be available for curling and skating this winter.

Social Functions

Initiation Ceremony in Partick Police Gymnasium on 17th November 1911. President James T. Ward welcomed the members in his well-known general fashion and provided creature comforts on a lavish scale. Captain James Watson acted as Initiating High Priest and administered the Curling Sacrament to the novices with much acceptance. In the presence of eighteen "made" curlers the following seventeen members were "made", taking the oath of secrecy and acknowledging themselves henceforth "keen keen curlers"—

Robert J. Borthwick	Hugh J. Craig
Geo. W. Duckett	Arthur Booth
Douglas Baird	William Sillery
William Cameron (Capt. of Police)	Matthew Reid
Robert L. Duncan	Thos. K. Ward
R. A. Smellie	Matthew White, Junr.
H. L. Arter	Alex. Craig
James Macintosh	Arch. Low (Partick Councillor)
John Gracie (Doctor of Medicine)	

"After the ceremony the newly made curlers attended the usual Court of Inquisition and submitted willingly to the customary ordeal. The arrangements and appliances were made or furnished by Chief-Dooker D. D. Gow, and were of the new complete and searching character. Mattha' White acted as examining Magistrate and bore the great brunt of Singer McColl's Smeek (intended for the candidates) with exemplary heroism. Davie Muirhead operated the chains with devilish ingenuity whilst Johnnie Campbell devoted untiring energy to assisting the candidates to climb over the broom. David Robinson's performance with the bell had the true Milkman's touch, and so enraptured John Stewart that at a later stage of the proceedings he mistook the bell for the Club's Trophy and proposed its health. All the other members assisted most heartily in administering delicate attentions to the blindfolded novices who on their part had no sooner recovered from their final plunge than they turned upon their fellow victims with great relish. The evening concluded with a square drink, in the course of which Col. W. B. Johnston proposed the health of Captain Watson in an interesting and felicitous speech. Speeches of an ambiguous nature by Sandy Craig and anecdotal character by George Duckett were also made. The Secretary, in proposing the health of universal provider Davie Gow, alluded to the great trouble he had been at in preparing for the ceremony. Davie suitably responded and convulsed the assembly with an imitation of a speech by an ex-M.P. for Partick. After the President had been inadequately thanked for the kind and thoughtful way in which he had presided over all the doings of the night, and a message of sympathy sent to the ex-President, Hunter Kennedy, who had not yet recovered from a very severe illness, the meeting broke up with 'Auld Lang Syne' before 11 o'clock."

Club Dinner, 20th December 1911—In Grand Hotel, Glasgow. In this Anno Domini 1970 it is of interest to note the costs of this sumptuous meal in one of Glasgow's then well-appointed hotels, just recently levelled to the ground to make way for the new inner circle road from Anderston to Port Dundas.

"Tickets 5/6d. each which included five bottles of Lang's Liqueur Whisky at 6/0d. and five syphons of Schweppes soda. Hotel price 4/6d. each including a nip with the Haggis, and a good piano; and 5/0d. added for Special Licence extending hour from 10 o'clock till midnight.''

BILL O' FARE
"Mak road-metal o' it"
Soups

Cockie Leekie   Scotch Broth
"Hatched in Partick"   "Draw the pot-lid"

Fish
"From our own Pond"
Grilled Loch Fyne Herrings
"Partick Councillors"

The Haggis
"Time for a dram"

Joints
"Don't be a hog"
Curlers' Beef and Greens   Roast Leg of Mutton
"Ne'er a Kowe"   "Crack an Egg on't"

Sweets
"Cuddle into them"
Plum Pudding   Apple Tart
"Stones on the dour side"   "Canadian Trophy"

Cheese Straws
"Soop them aff, lads"

Coffee
"Close the port"
and
"Kiggle Kaggle to and fro"

A copy of this "Bill o' Fare" interspersed with gleanings from the rink is attached to the minute, and is headed by a reproduction of a photograph of the then new rink, with Balshagray Avenue, as it then was, in the background and a dozen of more members and their stones on the frozen pond.

11th March 1914—A Curlers' Court was held in Partick Police Gymnasium when seventeen members were duly "made" by Captain James Watson, viz.:

W. R. Duckett	James Maitland	G. G. Henderson
A. J. Kemp	W. J. Dodd	A. G. Hunter
Geo. Paterson	Robert Scott	Thos. Duncan
James Craig	W. F. McAusland	John W. Lawrie
Thos. Hamilton	James Curdie	H. J. Clerk
John Stewart	W. Brock	

"*Taking no Risks*", story from a Royal Club Annual about this time.

"A curler who was in the habit of appearing on the rink with his ears covered by the flaps of his cap one day appeared with the flaps up. Questioned as to the change, he said, 'I havena pit the lugs doon since my accident.' 'Accident!' rejoined his questioner, 'I never heard tell o't, I hope ye werene muckle hurt.' 'Weel, no,' replied the curler, 'It was this way. The Laird said to me ae day, "Will ye tak a dram?" and the lugs were doon, sae I didn't hear him!' "

1920-1930

ABOUT this time there was a proposal to build an ice rink at Pitt Street but this fell through owing to lack of financial support. The suggestion was then made that a rink for curlers and skaters should be included in the new Kelvin Hall which was then under construction. The 10th Province took this up with the Corporation without success but Hunter Kennedy pursued the idea with energy and was instrumental in getting a syndicate to purchase the old ice rink at Crossmyloof and a company was formed to reconstruct it at a cost of £21,500.

At a Committee Meeting on 4th September 1922, a letter was read suggesting the Club change to the Glasgow Province. It was unanimously agreed and the Secretary was instructed to reply that in view of our long association with the 10th Province we prefer to remain in that Province. On 1st December following, the President reported that he had a good deal of correspondence with the Secretary of the R.C.C.C. regarding the proposed change to the Glasgow Province and read a letter dated 20th November from the Secretary of the R.C.C.C. reading "I had your letter of 18th inst. and in the circumstances you mention I am authorised to include Partick Club in the 10th Province". This was heartily received and a special vote of thanks was awarded to the President for the great trouble he had in connection with this matter.

At a Committee Meeting held on 28th January 1929, the President reported ladies were forming Curling Clubs at Crossmyloof, likely to be arranged in districts. He thought it might be considered a source of revenue that a Ladies' Club be formed to have the use of the Club ice during the day, say from 10 am. to 4 p.m. After discussion it was agreed to allow the latter to lie over for consideration meantime. It continues to lie!

The Large Pond Trouble

The leakage from the Large Pond was a source of continual trouble all through this decade. This was known at the end of the war when it is mentioned in the minute of the A.G.M. 8th October 1918. The President then said the pond required re-puddling, "which was impossible at present". In October 1921 the Vice-President offered to get an estimate to divide the pond in an endeavour to get a reduced area made tight. In the following

September a report by Mr. J. A. Warren and Mr. G. A. Campbell stated that it would cost about £25, while the Parks Superintendent offered to have drain pipes examined. This was done and a new outlet valve fitted. During 1922 Mr. Bannatyne was consulted, but could not suggest anything, while the Parks Superintendent agreed to have a roller put over it after the hay was cut. But there was no improvement and during 1924 the President and Vice-President had a meeting with the Parks Superintendent and sug-gested to him that the trouble was probably due to agricultural operations by the Corporation during the war, to which he agreed. He promised to have the pond thoroughly examined and to endeavour to discover the cause of the leakage. Negotiations went on through 1926 with Mr. Matthews, the new Parks Superintendent, who would not admit that his Department were in any way responsible, and in 1927-28 the President had interviews and correspondence with several Councillors to induce the Corporation to do something to repair the leak. However, at the A.G.M., 19th October 1928, the President read a letter from the Town Clerk-Depute stating the Corporation were not prepared to do anything. During later years the Club made attempts, by reducing the area, to make a portion watertight, but these endeavours do not seem to have had any success.

That the rink was right and available for curling prior to the war goes without saying; that the puddled bottom of the rink was turned over and greatly disturbed by the Corporation for the purpose of growing vegetables is not denied; and that thereafter it was never capable of holding water, nor of any use as a curling rink, in spite of the trouble taken by the Club and its office-bearers and of the expenses of trying to remedy the trouble—all gives the impression that the Club did not at that time get a fair deal. Thus from the years 1914-18 till now the Club has never had the use of this pond, which it made in 1893, when the first lease was entered into with the Burgh Council of Partick.

It is to be hoped that the recent (1968) major operations and alterations at the north-east corner of Victoria Park will not have rendered the remaining artificial shallow rink of the Club incapable of holding water. Such a result from all the bulldozing and changing of levels for the new wide access road through the east end of Victoria Park to the Whiteinch Tunnel may well be expected. If so it is hoped the powers that be will repair any resulting damage, which, though a trivial item in the total cost of these great works, could be quite beyond the resources of the Club, a leaseholder of the Corporation.

Hacks

At Committee Meeting at the President's residence, John M. Lamont suggested it would be a good thing if members had an opportunity of practising playing off the hack at our own pond. He had endeavoured to get some of these at the ice rink, but had failed to do so. Mr. Hunter Kennedy then offered to supply the Club with a pair, and the meeting thanked him for his generous offer.

The Treasurer's report in October 1928 showed a debit balance of £30.9/7d. due to abnormal expenditure on the rinks and other repairs. By increased membership, generosity of members, and sale of stones this deficit was converted to a credit balance of £18.3/5d. by the Annual General Meeting in October 1929. Throughout the ten-year period the annual subscription remained at 15/0d.

Office-Bearers

Honorary Member—1921 Captain Watson.

Life Member—D. Muirhead.

Presidents—1920 Robert Robinson, 1921-28 John M. Lamont, 1929 David Robinson.

Vice-Presidents—1920 J. M. Lamont, 1921-29 John A. Warren.

Representative Members 1920-29 Hunter Kennedy, 1920-21 W. E. McColl, 1922-26 D. Muirhead, 1927-29 Jas. T. Ward.

Treasurer—1920-29 H. J. McIntosh.

Hon. Secretary—1920-23 R. A. Smellie, 1924-29 H. J. Craig.

Match Secretary—1920-28 Jas. Craig, 1921-29 R. J. Borthwick.

Honorary Chaplains—1920-24 Rev. A. W. Stevenson, 1925-28 Rev. P. C. Millar, O.B.E., B.D., 1929 Rev. J. Mitchell Kerr.

Ice Master—1929 T. C. Alexander.

Regular Members

James Watson	J. T. Ward	Thomas Duncan
Matthew White	William Kennedy	R. J. Borthwick
D. D. Gow	J. G. Kennedy	Robert Paul
Robt. Duncan	W. Ward	R. A. Smellie
William McColl	M. H. Kennedy	Jas. Stuart
J. M. Lamont	David Robinson	John A. Warren
D. Muirhead	S. Mechan	H. J. McIntosh
Robert Robinson		

Occasional Members—Thirty-three, including M. Robinson, Major Dr. F. Gracie, Captain Dr. J. Gracie, H. I. Craig, Dr. A. E. Ward, Lt. Thos. K. Ward, Jas. Curdie, T. C. Alexander, W. P. Weir, Geo. McColl.

Grand Matches and Province Bonspiels

Scotland v. England International, played at Edinburgh Ice Rink on 14th-15th March 1923. Scotland won by 125 shots. M. Hunter Kennedy (Partick) was one of the players.

In the Royal Club Annual of 1925-26 there is a story headed "Come to my cowe". A Lothian skip, directing one of his players of the name of Bull, on one occasion created some amusement by saying, "Bull, come to my Kowe!"

Dumbartonshire (Tenth) Province Bonspiel, on 28th November 1925, at Loch Ardinning. Weather fine and ice keen and clear, but a strong wind from the nor-west made conditions difficult. It was the first bonspiel for thirteen years. Winners were East Kilpatrick two rinks, 13 up average; second, Duntocher one rink, 10½ up; third, Strathblane two rinks, 5 up average; Partick three rinks, skipped by J. G. Kennedy, M. H. Kennedy and Robert Craig, won 8 down average. The minute gives full report from *The Bulletin* of Monday, 30th November, with picture.

Grand Match on 4th December 1925, at Carsbreck. The Club was represented by only one rink. J. M. Lamont (skip), D. Robinson, Dr. John Gracie and T. C. Alexander, drawn against a Hercules Club rink skipped by John W. Bell. The latter won by 24 shots to 12. Weather was fine, but ice dour. A very pleasant game, which the four Partick members who had the good fortune to be playing, greatly enjoyed notwithstanding the defeat.

Dunbartonshire Province v. Canadians—In Edinburgh, 13th January 1926. From Province Minute Book with excerpt from *Glasgow Herald.* "Another victory for the Canadian Curlers signalised the morning's play at the Edinburgh Ice Rink yesterday. The Canadians had a majority of 37 shots over the Peeblesshire (six rinks aside). In the evening Dumbartonshire Curlers (six rinks) met the Canadians, and were beaten by 109 shots to 56. Partick rink included M. H. Kennedy (skip), J. M. Lamont, J. G. Kennedy and J. Ward. A joint dinner at the expense of the two provinces afterwards took place in the N.B. Station Hotel. Sir Henry Ballantine, President of the Peeblesshire Province, occupied the chair. A letter from Mr. Kidston (10th Province), who was abroad, was read by Mr. Hunter Kennedy (Partick), reminiscent of Mr. Kidston's various visits to Canada and of his curling experiences there.''

Province Bonspiel on 30*th December* 1927, at Loch Ardinning. Report from province minute. Ice in splendid condition with a strong cold west wind. Strathblane Club won with score of 8¾ up average. Eleven clubs, comprising thirty-two rinks with 128 players, took part in the competition.

Province Bonspiel on 26th January 1929, at Loch Ardinning. Thirteen clubs were represented by thirty-four rinks. The Kirkwood Cup was won by Cardross (Claud A. Allan and Arch. McIntyre) with an average of 13 shots up per rink; Partick Club were second with 5½ shots up; and Campsie Glen third 5 shots up. News cutting giving details of the individual rink results:

Partick—J. M. Lamont 3 up v. Bearsden.

J. A. Warren 8 up v. Dumbarton.

A further *Province Bonspiel was held at Crossmyloof* Ice Rink on 1st March 1929 for a Cup presented by Claud A. Allan, and four prizes to the rink of the winning club having the highest majority of shots. The province minute of this competition, with a news cutting, gives the detailed results: Baldernock, two rinks, won with 15½ up per rink. Partick, three rinks, John A. Warren, 6 up v. Cawder House; John Lamont 6 up v. Luss and Arrochar; and M. H. Kennedy drew with East Kilpatrick. Thirty-six rinks took part.

Province Bonspiel on 22nd February 1930, at Loch Ardinning. Twenty rinks took part. Ice strong but dull. The winners of the Kirkwood Cup were Campsie Glen, average 24 up; second, Baldernock 16 up; third, Cawder House 14 up; fourth, Luss and Arrochar and Cardross, each 3 up; sixth, Cardross and Duntocher, each 2⅔ up. Others, Strathblane, Partick, Dumbarton, Bearsden, Helensburgh and Waterside Gartshore were down in that order.

One of the Royal Club's Annuals of this decade has a story of possible interest to members of the 10th Province headed "Leave that Bottle". "A curler, carrying in his coat pocket a bottle of what in the parlance of some old minutes of clubs is called 'aqua', was making as though to cross Loch Ardinning, which happened to be then covered with a rather precarious sheet of ice. 'Hey, man,' exclaimed a voice from the shore, 'are ye ettlin to gang over?'

'Aye,' was the answer. 'Weel,' rejoined the voice, 'step back in the first place and leave that bottle ahint ye.' "

Cuthbert Cup Competition, held at the Scottish Ice Rink on 4th April 1930. This was the first competition of this cup presented to the Province by T. S. Cuthbert for Annual Inside Ice Competition. First, Bearsden $9\frac{2}{3}$ shots up; second, East Kilpatrick 4 shots up; third, Luss and Arrochar 3 shots up; fourth, Baldernock $1\frac{2}{3}$; fifth, Duntocher $1\frac{1}{3}$. Four silver spoons presented by the Province were won by the rink skipped by J. M. Dykes, 15 shots up, being highest against their opponents.

"Bell" Competitions and other Club Games

24th October 1922. A Club Competition was held in Edinburgh Ice Rink to play for four enamelled badges presented by the President. Four rinks entered.

M. Hunter Kennedy (skip)		J. G. Kennedy (skip)	
Thos. K. Ward	12	Marcus Robinson	5
Robert Paul	shots v.	Dr. A. E. Ward	shots
H. J. McIntosh		J. A. Warren	
David Muirhead (skip)		James T. Ward	
Robert Duncan	14	H. J. Craig	8
Robert Craig	shots v.	Dr. Campbell	shots
W. L. Duncan		R. U. Borthwick	

Hunter Kennedy's rink won by 7 shots. The President kindly entertained the members to lunch on the way through and Marcus Robinson giving hospitality at tea on completion of the game.

5th December 1925. "The Bell" Competition was played on the shallow pond on this Saturday at 11.0 a.m. and afternoon finishing about 4.15 when a meeting was held in the clubhouse.

The President intimated that J. Forrest's was the highest up, but as he was not a member, he could not hold the "Bell". After some discussion, the Committee agreed that the handsome brooches presented by the President be handed over to the other three members of J. Forrest's rink, Robert Robinson, W. M. Bremmer and T. C. Alexander, that the present match be played on the first available opportunity, the remaining brooch going to the winning skip together with custody of the "Bell". (There is no minute of this postponed match having taken place).

A Curlers' Court was held on 15th February 1929 in the Partick Police Gymnasium.

1930-1940

This period started with a financial crisis in the country, when the Government threw in their hands and a coalition Government was formed to carry on the administration. The crisis followed some years of considerable unemployment in the steel, shipbuilding, engineering and other heavy industries, causing much industrial unrest. During the early thirties Hitler in Germany and Mussolini in Italy started their sabre-rattling, and their making, and later breaking, of treaties, all culminating in war in 1939.

At the Annual General Meeting of the Club on 9th October 1930 —present, the President, Vice-President, Robert Paul, H. J. Macintosh, R. J. Borthwick, W. Cameron, R. Roxburgh, J. Duncan Cran, J. Y. Moyes, Jas. Anderson, Robert Craig, T. C. Alexander, James Jackson, W. Calder Brown, J. Reid, W. Barclay, Arthur Hadden and H. J. Craig—the Secretary referred to the generosity of the President in taking down and re-erecting the electric rink lamps and of F. C. McGillivray and James Miller in supplying coals for the clubhouse, and of David Bennie for his gift of rope hawsers as buffers at the rink ends. The question of admitting ladies as members was raised, but after discussion it was resolved not to do so meantime. In 1932 a new ten year lease of the ground was obtained from the Corporation, and the three members—John M. Lamont, David Robinson and John A. Warren—who had carried through the negotiations were thanked for their services and author-ised to sign the Minute of Agreement for and on behalf of the Club. Unsuccessful attempts were again made to stop the leaking from the large pond. During these years all A.G.M.s were held in the clubhouse, Balshagray Avenue; Committee meetings when not in the clubhouse in the smokeroom of Daniel Brown's restaurant in St. Vincent Street about 5.30 p.m., which better suited members on their way home. At a Committee on 6th December 1933, the President, H. J. Craig, drew attention to a letter in the *Glasgow Herald* from the Chaplain to the Royal Club in which he suggested clubs should hold Church parades under their Club Chaplains. The meeting decided after discussion to "defer the matter for further consideration". The letter which had appeared in the *Herald* on 4th December is worthy of insertion here.

"Killearn Old Manse, Dumgoyne, December 1.

"*Curlers' Church Parades.* Sir, my personal opinion is favourable to such services, as your correspondent in 'Ice Rink Notes' suggests. I have sometimes wondered why such services are not more common than they are. Is it the influence of the words in the Catechism debarring 'thoughts about our wordly recreations' on the Lord's Day? Doubtless the old minister had these words in mind when he announced from the pulpit, 'My brethren, it's nae war speakin' it oot than thinkin' it in; if the frost holds I intend to be on the ice at ten o'clock the morn's morning'!

"Curlers are, I think, unique among sportsmen in appointing Chaplains. Is this not a consequence of their instructive recognition of the wealth of religious and spiritual instruction derivable from 'The matchless game that feeds the flame of brotherhood in man'?

"Why not have a 'Curlers' Sunday', not, of course, in the sense of curling on Sunday—fact which was charged against a Bishop of Orkney—but in the sense of a special service for curlers?

"We all know how fond St. Paul was of employing martial and stadial metaphors and imagery as vehicles of spiritual instruction. I venture with all reverence to imagine that, had curling been practised in his day, he would have resorted to the rink for material of much varied and powerful exhortation. Sermons on curling could not well be dull or dry, and would in all probability be clear, keen and edifying.

"Of course, services for curlers can, unofficially, be held and in point of fact are sometimes held—particularly, I think in the Dominion of Canada; but it is worth considering whether the Royal Club should not give its imprimature to the holding of such.

"If present at the next Annual Meeting of the Club I am prepared to suggest that, in the absence of objections from the various international ecclesiastical authorities concerned, it be a standing recommendation to the Chaplains of local clubs to hold Annual Church Parades of Curlers. It is the glory of the game of curling to appeal at once to that love of contention which is inherent in mankind and to the fraternal instincts of humanity. Curlers are *hostes attamen fratres*.

"I am, etc.,
"A Gordon Mitchell, D.D.,
Chaplain, R.C.C.C."

There is no further reference in the minutes to that matter deferred "for further consideration" on 6th December 1933. However, one of the older Club members recollects being present at a Church service and finds in his notes that it was conducted by the Club Chaplain, the Rev. J. Mitchell Kerr, B.D., in his church, Woodside Parish, Great Western Road, Glasgow, at 6.30 p.m. on 7th November 1937. The preacher was the Rev. A. Gordon Mitchell, D.D. (Strathendrick C.C. and Chaplain to the Royal Club), who delivered an interesting topical address to a well attended congregation, which included a large number of Partick C.C. members, occupying several pews in the body of the church.

In 1938 there was a movement on foot to have a panel placed over the fireplace in the clubhouse with the names of the Presidents since the inauguration of the Club in 1842. At a Committee Meeting on 6th April the Secretary stated he had received a plywood panel for the purpose from Mr. David Bennie, and that he had made out a list of the past Presidents. He was instructed to get prices for the lettering of the same. Owing to the international developments thereafter, nothing more about it appears in the minute book.

The A.G.M. in October 1939 decided that all members serving in H.M. Forces be relieved of paying the annual subscription, which remained at 15/0d. through the period. It was also agreed that should there be ice on any Saturday during the season, and a sufficient number of members turn out, the competition for the "Partick Bell" should be carried through.

The Centenary of the Royal Caledonian Curling Club was celebrated by the holding of a dinner in the Music Hall, Edinburgh, on 27th July 1938. President The Duke of Athol in the chair. There were four hundred gentlemen present, but no mention of a representative from Partick C.C. either in the R.C.'s report of this function or in the Club's minutes. This is surprising as the Club, through its hundred years very regularly has been represented at the Annual and other Special Meetings of the R.C. The Council of the R.C. decided to commemorate the Centenary by presenting a Special Silver Medal to all the clubs which had been members continuously from the beginning. It was also agreed that similar medals be given in future to clubs attaining a hundred years of continuous membership. Seventeen clubs qualified and were there and then presented with the medals. The Partick C.C. has been the proud possessor of this silver medal since 1942.

Office-Bearers
Honorary Members—From 1930 Jas. T. Ward and the Rt. Hon.

Lord Provost Kelly, from 1935 John M. Lamont, 1938 A. S. L. Young, M.P.

Presidents—1930 David Robinson, 1931-32 John A. Warren, 1933-34 H. J. Craig, 1935-36 Dr. John Gracie, 1937-39 Wilson Robinson.

Vice-Presidents—1930 John A. Warren, 1931 Robert Craig, 1932 H. J. Craig, 1933-34 Dr. John Gracie, 1935-36 Wilson Robinson, 1937-39 J. K. Ward.

Representative Members—1930 M. Hunter Kennedy and John M. Lamont, 1931-33 John M. Lamont and David Robinson, 1934 John M. Lamont and J. A. Warren, 1935-36 John A. Warren and H. J. Craig, 1937-39 H. J. Craig and Dr. John Gracie.

Chaplain—1930-39 Rev. J. Mitchell Kerr, B.D.

Hon. Treasurer—H. J. McIntosh, 1932-39 D. M. McFarlane.

Hon. Secretary—H. J. Craig, 1932-39 T. C. Alexander.

Ice-Masters—1930-32 T. C. Alexander, 1933 J. D. Cran, 1934-39 R. J. Borthwick.

Regular Members—from R.C. Annual 1931-32

J. M. Lamont	T. C. Alexander	H. J. McIntosh
Robert Robinson	David Robinson	Wilson Robinson
James Craig	R. J. Borthwick	H. J. Craig
J. K. Ward	Robert Paul	A. D. Hislop
James Jackson	John Reid	R. Roxburgh
J. G. Kennedy	Dr. John Gracie	Jas. Watson
Robert Craig	John A. Warren	Jas. Anderson
W. Cameron		

During this period the Club lost several members who had given yeoman service and it is worth while recording here some of the details about them.

James T. Ward was a member for over thirty years, serving as President from 1910 to 1912, as Match Secretary 1912 to 1919 and as Representative Member from 1927 to 1929. He was a very skilful curler who skipped in Royal Club and Open Competitions and played for Scotland in Canada and at home.

Hunter Kennedy was another distinguished worthy who died suddenly one evening on his way to curl at Crossmyloof. A well-known Rugby player in his youth, he was taught to curl by his uncle "Long John" Anderson, himself an expert player. With his brother Johnny he presented to the Club the clubhouse at Partick and helped to reline the two ponds forming the rinks there. He also built a rink at Carrbridge when he was working there as a Civil Engineer. He was well known in international curling circles, having toured with teams in Canada and went regularly to play in Switzerland. He was a President of the 10th Province and a member of the R.C.C.C. Council and one of the curlers responsible for the resuscitation of Crossmyloof.

John Lamont and David Robinson can be bracketed together because these were the two who kept the Club alive at a time when it nearly ceased to exist and its finances were in a very perilous state. They both filled the offices of Treasurer, Secretary and President and spared no effort to promote curling and the interests of Partick over a long period of years.

Social Functions

Curlers' Grace by the Rev. F. S. Gordon Fraser, Old Parish Church, Nairn; from Royal Club Annual 1938-39.

> "Lord, by whose mercy we are here
> As brithers all o' ane accord
> As thou dost bless oor hame an' gear
> Noo bless oor Curlers' festive board.
>
> "As keen the ice an' clear the day,
> Sae clean we pray oor hearts may be
> That, as the game o' life we play
> We a' the while may throw for Thee."

Curlers' Court. An Initiation Ceremony and Court was held in the hall of the "Knights of St. Columba", Partick Cross Subway, on Friday, 10th November 1933. When a court of seventeen members assembled under "My Lord" J. Mitchell Kerr, with officers R. J. Borthwick and T. C. Alexander in attendance. The ceremony was carried out by "My Lord" with dignity and efficiency, and on the rising of this Court the whole company sat down to supper, when the fun was fast and furious. The following eighteen members were duly initiated as curlers:

J. Duncan Cran	Jas. A. Lyle	Jas. Jackson
W. B. Renwick	Chas. Watters, Largs	John Y. Moyes
W. Foulds Martin, Jun.	Jas. Pattison	Jas. M. Cameron
George Watson	W. Cameron	Isaac D. Scott
D. M. McFarlane	John Shearer	J. McNicoll Reid
Alex. D. Hislop	J. C. Mustard	George Smellie

Curlers' Court and Initiation Ceremony was held in the hall of the "Knights of St. Columba", Partick Cross Subway, on Friday, 19th February 1937, when a court of eighteen members assembled under "My Lord" Rev. J. Mitchell Kerr with officers T. C. Alexander and R. J. Borthwick in attendance. The ceremony was carried out by "My Lord" with great dignity, and on the rising of the court the whole company sat down to the festive board, where free and unconstrained joviality prevailed. Eleven curlers were duly initiated as follows:

George Duncan	Joseph Cousland	Douglas Macarthur
David W. Robinson	James Methvem	Horace Bennett
James B. Helm	J. Morris McIndoe	Robert S. Pattison
Ralph A. Rolland	R. M. Nelson	

1939—*Full List of Club Members*

As the 1938-39 Annual of the Royal Club was the last issued before the 1939-45 War started, and contained a complete list of all regular and occasional members in the clubs at that time, it seems a proper ending to this decade to give the full list.

Honorary Members

Sir Thomas Kelly, LL.D., Rev. J. Mitchell Kerr, B.D., A. S. L. Young, M.P.

Regular Members

Robert Robinson	John A. Warren	H. D. Campbell
James Craig	Wilson Robinson	J. Duncan Cran
J. N. Ward	H. J. Craig	J. Shearer
James Jackson	A. D. Hislop	J. Methven
J. G. Kennedy	Joseph Cousland	W. Foulds Martin
Robert Craig	Dr. John Gracie	Jas. A. Lyle
T. C. Alexander	W. Cameron	I. D. Scott
R. N. Borthwick	R. Allan Ogg	Wm. Gardner.

Occasional Members

Thos. C. Reid	Geo. Duncan	J. C. Hamilton
G. B. Tennant	William Lyle	Alex. Kennedy
D. F. Bennie	Murray Niven	J. Todd
John Y. Moyes	A. M. O. Robertson	A. A. H. Douglas
Dr. H. M. Calder	Allan Robertson	Dr. E. M. Cumming
Jas. Pattison	W. R. Campbell	Jas. Miller
J. N. Macnie	Ian Moyes	W. G. Brown

D. M. McFarlane	J. Horace Bennett	J. Headrick Ross
J. Crowley	William Barclay	J. Gray
D. W. Robinson	Jas. Taylor	Dr. Stewart
W. Duckett	M. Russell White	Jas. Watson
J. B. McOuat	Arch. McFarlane	K. Campbell
T. D. Carpenter	T. W. Ward	Geo. E. Watson
S. Cunningham	Jas. Ritchie, C.B.E.	A. S. Brown
Rev. J. Mitchell Kerr	Douglas Rennie	Chas. E. Bell

1940-1950

THIS decade started with the country at war with Hitler's Germany, though not yet in the Autumn of 1940 fully geared to the all embracing and world-wide conflict which it became. The next five years till 1945 were fully taken up in recovering the territories over-run by the enemy and thereafter occupying and taking possession of his countries and their capital cities. This called for a stupendous all-out effort—armed forces built up and fully equipped for meeting and defeating the enemy on land and sea and in the air. The inhabitants, men and women of Partick, as of every part of the United Kingdom, were, directly or indirectly, working towards that end. Those with any leisure or free time joined the Home Guard, the Special Constables, the Air Raid Precautions Depots, or other Auxiliary Services according to their age sex and ability. To meet the need of healthy outdoor exercise for those in sedentary and indoor occupations, the local authority or Corporation continued to provide and maintain facilities in the Public parks, and the clubs to do the same for their members.

The young members of the Partick Curling Club were all away with the forces, and consequently the average age of those able to take advantage of the clubs' facilities and of attending meetings was high. Moreover, because of the very restricted lighting after sundown, meetings were held on Saturday afternoons, generally without a quorum of members present. These meetings unanimously agreed to carry on their business subject to confirmation at the next A.G.M.

At such meetings in 1940–41 the Hon. Secretary reported a number of curling sessions were played in daylight on excellent ice. At the A.G.M. in 1942 it was intimated that the ground lease would expire on Whitsunday, 1943, and a sub-committee, composed of the President, H. J. Craig and the Hon. Secretary was appointed to negotiate a renewal of the lease.

The A.G.M. of 1943 heard with deep regret of the deaths of Captain R. Allan Ogg, H.L.I.; Major Ian Moyes, R.E.M.E.; Flt. Lieut. T. W. Ward, R.A.F.; and of W. Cameron, member, the members present, upstanding in token of respect. The names of the first three of those appear in the Royal Club Annual 1944–45 as Partick C.C. members who died on Active Service.

From the Autumn of 1944, after the successful landings and

operations in France, and the pushing of the enemy northwards from Churchill's "Under-belly of Europe", restive members of the club began to agitate the office-bearers for some sign of a return to the old pursuits. At the A.G.M. on 7th October the Hon. Secretary reported he had been in touch with the Chief Constable regarding lights at the pond, but was informed no permission could be given. He had also approached Mr. Frank Stuart, a Director of the Ice Rink Co. at Crossmyloof. His reply was to keep in touch and apply as soon as the opening of the Rink was advertised.

The 1945 A.G.M. was held at the Clubhouse on Saturday afternoon 5th October. The President drew attention to the fact that we met under much more happy circumstances than for several years, in that Victory had been achieved in the World War and we had now to settle down to a Peace Policy. The Hon. Secretary reported that the Ice Rink at Crossmyloof was expected to be derequisitioned soon or in the near future. The meeting then arranged to have the pond lights re-erected, the pond cleaned and heads marked and painted. The Representative Member, H. J. Craig had attended the Royal Club Meeting in Edinburgh and reported. The Secretary was instructed to write to Sir A. S. L. Young, Bart., M.P. for Partick and congratulate him on the Honour of a Baronetcy conferred on him.

At the Annual General Meeting in 1947 the Representative Member was able to report that the Royal Caledonian Curling Club had upheld the Club's request to remain a member of the Tenth (Dunbartonshire) Province and not to be made a member of Glasgow Province as recorded in the Journal. This enabled the Club to carry on their traditions which had begun when Partick was outside the boundary of Glasgow.

The Tenth Province was at this time suffering a hiatus which is oft to befall all curling clubs from time to time. During the War the office of Secretary had become vacant due to the death of the Secretary, William Latta. Matters came to a head when arrangements were being made for the visit of a team of Canadian Curlers to Scotland in 1950. Under pressure from the Secretary of the Royal Club, David Robinson, the Honorary Secretary of the Partick Club agreed to convene a meeting of some of the Clubs who had formed the Province in the pre-war years under the chairmanship of George Reid a member of the R.C.C.C. Council. The meeting was attended by representatives of Bearsden, Campsie

Glen, Dumbarton, Cardross, Helensburgh and Glasgow Academical Clubs. Rinks were chosen to play against the Canadians and the opportunity was taken to resuscitate Province competitions and John Filshie (Dumbarton) was elected President, John McIntyre (Cardross) Vice-President and David Robinson (Partick) Hon. Secretary. Various trophies were traced and have been played for annually during the following twenty years with great keenness and enjoyment by Dunbartonshire curlers.

Office-Bearers

At the A.G.M. 1940 there were re-elected for the duration of the War Hon. Members—Sir Thos. Kelly and A. S. L. Young, M.P. for Partick. President Wilson Robinson; Vice-President J. K. Ward; Chaplain Rev. J. Mitchell Kerr; Hon. Treasurer D. M. McFarlane; Hon. Secretary T. C. Alexander.

	1945–6 A.G.M. 6.10.45	1946–7 A.G.M. 5.10.46	1947–8 A.G.M. 3.10.47	1948–9 A.G.M. 1.10.48	1949–50 A.G.M. 20.9.49
President:	T. K. Ward	D. Bennie	T. C. Alexander	J. D. Cran	A. D. Hislop
Vice-Pres.:	D. Bennie	J. D. Cran	J. D. Cran	T. G. Robinson	T. G. Robinson
Chaplain:	Rev. Eric P. Hind	Rev. Eric P. Hind	Rev. Eric P. Hind	Rev. J. Hay Hamilton	Rev. J. Hay Hamilton
Hon. Pres.:	D. M. McFarlane	D. M. McFarlane	D. M. McFarlane	D. M. McFarlane	D. M. McFarlane
Hon. Sec.:	T. C. Alexander	D. W. Robinson	D. W. Robinson	D. W. Robinson	D. W. Robinson
Rep. Members:	H. J. Craig	H. J. Craig	J. D. Cran	T. C. Alexander	T. C. Alexander
	J. D. Cran	J. D. Cran	H. D. Campbell	H. D. Campbell	J. D. Cran
Ice Master:	H. D. Campbell	H. D. Campbell	G. C. Graham		
Committee	M. Niven	A. D. Hislop	G. Kidd	D. Carnegie	J. K. Craig
	W. Robinson	R. S. Pattison	D. R. Edward	H. J. Craig	W. F. Roxburgh
			T. G. Robinson		

List of Regular Members in R.C. Annual 1948–49

T. C. Alexander	George C. Graham	Wilson Robinson
J. Duncan Cran	R. H. Kidd	R. A. Smellie
R. A. French	J. R. McCrae	J. Kirke Craig
Gordon Kidd	T. G. Robinson	John Duncan
J. A. Lyle	A. C. Rutherford	A. D. Hislop
J. G. Robinson	H. J. Craig	George Laird
W. F. Roxburgh	J. Cousland	D. W. Robinson
T. S. Weston	Rev. J. Hay Hamilton	G. R. Roxburgh
D. Carnegie	J. Kirkhope	J. M. Steven
H. D. Campbell	D. M. McFarlane	R. S. Pattison

Occasional Members from Club Minutes

D. Edwards	John Gordon	W. A. P. Jack
George Duncan	J. T. Dowling	John G. Stenhouse
Prof. Ian Macdonald	Mungo B. Campbell	E. M. Kerr
Donald Currie	E. W. C. Alexander	Lt. Col. A. C. W.
R. N. Mills	A. Bruce McLean	May
Col. J. G. McKellar	Hector Thompson	P. J. McVoy
W. F. Knox	W. E. Hogg	J. A. R. Moffat
W. B. Miller	D. W. Clow	J. K. Hood
John McKay		Major H. L. Ewing

Matches and Competitions

There were no Grand Matches during the period.

Dunbartonshire (Tenth Province) and Open Competitions

December 1947—R.C.C.C. Rink Championship at Crossmyloof—First Round v. East Kilbride, who won 16–10. Rink—J. D. Cran, H. J. Craig, Dan McFarlane and A. D. Hislop (Skip).

1948–49—Crossmyloof Ice Rink Championship—A. D. Hislop (Skip). First round beat Falkirk (R. Young)17–12; second round lost to Waterside (J. Garvin) 5–15, R.C.C.C. Rink Championship (A. D. Hislop, Skip)—First round beat Durisdeer 12–10; second round lost to Braidwood (J. Gilchrist) 7–12. Team—J. K. Craig, D. W. Robinson, J. A. Lyle, Dan McFarlane.

Pairs Competition at Crossmyloof—A. D. Hislop and D. W. Robinson. First round and bye; second round lost to Ayr (W. Smith).

Stirling Maxwell Trophy—Played 7, won 2 and lost 5— points 4 (teams included: H. J. Craig (Skip), J. D. Cran (Skip), Geo. Duncan, Wilson Robinson, H. D. Campbell and Dan McFarlane).

1949–50—Kandersteg Cup—First round v. Kilmabreck—Lost 5–10. Team: W. F. Roxburgh, G. Kidd, J. K. Craig, A. D. Hislop (Skip).

Scottish Ice Rink Club Championships—Two rinks. First round a bye; second round v. Largs Thistle—Lost 15–30. Teams: W. R. Campbell, Geo. Duncan, D. McFarlane, J. D. Cran (Skip), down 8–12. Mr. F. Roxburgh, John Duncan, D. W. Robinson, A. D. Hislop (Skip), 7–18. Second round v. Ayr—Lost 8–13. Team: D. McFarlane, T. G. Robinson, J. D. Cran, A. D. Hislop (Skip).

Harrogate Trophy—First round v. Lanark—Lost 6–15. Team: J. A. Lyle, D. W. Robinson, A. D. Hislop, J. D. Cran (Skip).

E

Crossmyloof Club Championship—First round lost to Erskine 10–11. Team J. K. Craig, W. B. Miller, J. D. Cran, D. R. Edward (Skip).

31st January 1950. As mentioned above Dumbartonshire Province and Forth and Endrick Province each provided three rinks to play the Canadian visiting team on this date at Crossmyloof. Three Partick players were chosen to play in No. 2 Dunbartonshire rink: Dan McFarlane, Duncan Cran and A. D. Hislop with W. R. Filshie (Dumbarton) Skip. The Canadians won, but there is no record of the result in the Province Minutes. After the match the visitors were entertained to lunch in the Ice Rink Restaurant by the joint hosts. The Duke of Montrose kindly presided and made a short speech of welcome, to which one of the Canadians replied.

23rd February, 1950—A combined competition for the Cuthbert Cup and Claud Allan Medal was held at Crossmyloof, the Cup to be decided by the first round, highest up rink over their opponents, was won by Campsie Glen from Dumbarton (17–2). Partick rink: W. F. Roxburgh, W. R. Campbell, D. W. Robinson, A. D. Hislop (Skip) lost to Cawder House (9–13). The Claud Allan Medal was won by Campsie Glen from Glasgow Academicals (10–8) in the third (final) round.

District Medals

v. Dumbarton on 6th February 1948 at Crossmyloof—Two rinks a side.

A. D. Hislop (Skip) 14 v. M. Howie 13.

H. J. Craig (Skip) 14 v. W. R. Filshie 14. Partick won by 1 shot.

v. Port Glasgow on 8th February 1950—Partick won by 22–15.

Rinks—G. R. Roxburgh, G. C. Graham, J. K. Craig and J. D. Cran (Skip) 1 down.

W. F. Roxburgh, G. Kidd, J. A. Lyle, D. M. McFarlane (Skip) 8 up.

Inter-club Game v. Glasgow Academicals on 16th December 1947. Two rinks a side, at Crossmyloof: Partick win 26–15. T. C. Alexander 13 and J. E. W. Dallachy 10; and W. F. Martin 13 v. John Cowie 5.

Club Games

28th March 1947—"Bell" Competition—Ice available for only four rinks. Winners: W. F. Martin (Skip), J. D. Cran, D. McFarlane and H. J. Craig. Twenty-three shots from A. D. Hislop 5; other rink Wilson Robinson lost to T. D. Carpenter (4–14). Dinner after in Ice Rink Restaurant.

2nd March 1948—"Bell" Competition. Eight rinks entered. Winners J. G. McKellar, D. W. Robinson and W. F. Martin, J. D. Cran (Skip) v. J. A. Lyle rink; second 6 shots up D. Carnegie, v. J. Cousland; third 5 up A. D. Hislop v. D. M. McFarlane; fourth 4 up T. D. Carpenter v. H. D. Campbell. Dinner after in the Ice Rink Restaurant. Thirty-one members present. The President presented Balmoral bonnets to the winners, and Ex-President David Bennie cigarettes to the runners up.

12th April 1948—Points Game at Crossmyloof—a disappointing turn out. Dan McFarlane won an extra end after a tie of 16 shots each with George Kidd; T. C. Alexander and W. F. Martin 13 each; D. R. Edward 12.

28th October 1948—Two rinks game with Clydesdale Bank—Partick lost 10 down. T. C. Alexander rink 5 up; J. D. Cran rink 15 down.

25th March 1949—"Bell" Competition at Crossmyloof, eight rinks entered. Winners 9 shots up: A. D. Hislop (skip) D. R. Edward, John Duncan and G. C. Graham v. D. W. Robinson's rink; second Wilson Robinson v. T. G. Robinson; third W. F. Martin v. Dan McFarlane; fourth D. Carnegie v. T. C. Alexander. Dinner was served in the Ice Rink Restaurant after the Competition and most of the players took part. The President welcomed the Padre and H. J. Craig who was making his first appearance after his accident. The President's prizes of pewter mugs suitably inscribed were presented to the winning rink with a few fitting remarks from the President. Speeches were also made by the winning skip, the Hon. Secretary and David Carnegie who proposed the health of the President. The evening concluded with the singing of Lang Syne.

31st March 1950—"Bell" Competition. Winners: J. F. Martin (Skip), J. K. Craig v. R. A. Smellie and A. M. O. Robertson 6 up v. R. A. French rink; second J. D. Craig rink 5 up v. D. McFarlane; third T. C. Alexander 4 up v. D. Edward; fourth W. F. Roxburgh 1 up v. R. S. Pattison. After the match all adjourned to the Dowanhill House, Byres Road, Partick where the Club's centenary dinner was held with the President A. D. Hislop in the Chair.

Social Meetings

22nd October 1948. The Club held a "Curlers" Court in the Police Gymnasium, Beith Street, Partick, when the following twelve members were initiated by "My Lord" T. C. Alexander, assisted by "IIis Officers" W. Foulds Martin and David M. Robinson.

J. Gordon Robinson	John Kirkhope
Thomas G. Robinson	G. C. Graham
David Carnegie	W. Farquhar Roxburgh
Gordon Kidd	Robert A. Smellie
H. Dudley Campbell	John Duncan
Robert H. Kidd	James M. Steven

The initiates were duly made Brother Curlers with the time-honoured ceremony, and thereafter all members enjoyed light refreshments, and happily paid up the penalties prescribed by the Court for their individual misinterpretations of its orders.

31st March 1950. After "The Bell" Competition on this date at Crossmyloof members to the number of forty-three gathered in Dowanhill House, Byres Road to celebrate the Centenary of the Club. The President, A. D. Hislop, occupied the chair and was in his usual good form. A Menu Card is inserted in the Minute Book, having been signed by all present, including John A. Warren then within a month of his ninetieth birthday. The Toast List:

The King	The President
Partick Curling Club	The President
The Royal Caledonian Curling Club	J. Cousland
Reply	J. D. Cran
Old Partick Bell and Mr. J. Ross	T. C. Alexander
Reply	Winning Skip (J. Foulds Martin)
The Chairman	T. G. Robinson
Reply	The Chair

It was an enthusiastic and highly successful function. (The frontispiece of the menu card was drawn up by J. D. C.)

The Canadian Tour in Scotland in January, 1950

As two or three members of the club had the fortune to take part in the Tenth Province match with the visitors at Crossmyloof, and the pleasure of being invited to Canadian Farewell Banquet in the Music Hall, George Street, Edinburgh on 2nd February, it seems proper that this unique function should be at least mentioned.

Men's memories are short, and it is difficult only twenty years after to recall to mind the "precise" rations per head per week of common articles of food to meet the average daily domestic needs, while many of these restrictions remained in force till after the date of this function. The Hosts modestly termed it a luncheon, but the article in the Royal Club Annual persistently and more appropriately described it as a banquet. Consequently those Scots guests, home-based during the previous ten years suddenly found themselves faced with a gargantuan gastronomic ordeal. This, compared to their normal diet, was certainly out of their hemisphere seemed as food for the gods! and was wonderfully served. For all this hospitality the Canadians were enthusiastically thanked by their guests.

The Royal Club Annual 1950–51 sums up "throughout this comprehensive tour the Canadians, fifty two in number, soon showed their merit both as curlers and as sportsmen. After the opening games our visitors were seldom defeated by any but our strongest rinks, and it is significant to note that Scotland only managed to retain possession of the Strathcona Cup by the narrow margin of 30 shots over a series of ten games.

At the close of the tour the Canadian teams united to throw a banquet in the Music Hall, Edinburgh, which was attended by about 400 curlers and their wives. The tourists had conceived the happy idea of bringing over all the foodstuffs for the banquet from Canada, and the different items on the menu were traditional Canadian.

This was a fitting finish to a most successful tour, and on the banquet a very powerful oration was delivered by the Hon. Errick F. Willis, Deputy Prime Minister of Manitoba and Captain of the Canadian Team." (The oration was reproduced in the same annual).

1950-1960

From the end of the war in 1945 an increase in membership was recorded till in 1952 the Annual Meeting resolved to stop the admission of new members. The revival of the Tenth Province in January, 1950 with its various trophies to be played for considerably added to the work of the Province Honorary Secretary, who at this time was David W. Robinson (Partick) and who, owing to the Province having been dormant for some ten years, had to re-organise these competitions and arrange ice for them at the Scottish Ice Rink. That he did so with remarkable efficiency for many years was readily acknowledged by the Office-bearers and secretaries of the Provincial Clubs.

During this post-war period old clubs had been increasing their membership, new clubs were being instituted, and ice rinks were inaugurating more open competitions. The resulting demand for ice was such that clubs were not being allotted so much ice as they applied for, nor their keen curling members as much play as they desired. Early in 1951 the President T. G. Robinson was anxious that more members should have opportunity of playing in the Provincial and other competitions, though the main difficulty was inability of young players to be available at times other than the evenings. During the seasons skips were appointed for Provincial and other competitions and generally were given authority to arrange their own rinks, though in Provincial and friendly matches with other clubs there was an understanding that as many members as possible should participate in these. This was frequently done by ballot at club meetings. A club league was more than once suggested, but it was not adopted till at the A.G.M. 1958 Eric McNaught (Hon. Secretary Elect) proposed another competition to provide added keenness within the club and thereby improve the standard of play. This was fully supported by the retiring Hon. Secretary and agreed for season 1959–60, the committee to make the necessary arrangements. The committee duly met, the President in the chair, and after discussion decided that a league competition be operated next session in groups of eight members, and that a new trophy in the form of a curling stone be procured. To enable prizes to be presented it was further agreed that an entry fee of 2/6d. per head be collected by the skips and handed over to the Treasurer. The draw for groups of eight members in each there and then took place, and the Hon. Secretary instructed to apply for the necessary ice at the Scottish Ice Rink. The League, having been in operation since then, has proved to be a most successful and sporting competition throughout each curling season—in short a good thing. Not only do the individual members in the groups each play their part in the games with all the other groups, but they take a direct interest in the progressively changing relative positions of the contesting group. They also tend to develop an increasingly sporting spirit, assessing the odds for and against their opponents, and therefrom deriving much fun as the season draws to a close and earlier leaders in the "League Stakes" are displaced by an unexpected back-marker with or without a little bit of luck!

Excerpts from the minutes of these years are of interest. At the Annual General Meeting on 29th September 1950. The revised Club Constitution and Rules were passed and authorised to be printed. At the A.G.M. 1951 The President read a letter from the Scottish Ice Rink Club intimating a proposal to open the Curling Rink on Sundays. The meeting unanimously decided not to support this but that, if any members wished to do so on their own, they were welcome to do so.

The President at the A.G.M. on 22nd September 1953, congratulated T. G. Robinson on his election as Chairman of the Glasgow Chamber of Commerce and on his discharge of that distinguished office. The Hon. Secretary reported that he had attended the Representative meeting of the Royal Club with Duncan Cran, who, he was pleased to say, had been elected after a vote to the Council of the Royal Club for the North-West area. It was unanimously decided to minute the clubs' congratulations on this appointment.

On 2nd April 1954 after "The Bell" competition, at the dinner in Dowanhill House, David Carnegie President in the chair, Robin Reid on behalf of Mrs. H. J. Craig presented to the club a silver Quaich, which had been gifted by her in memory of her husband. The President in accepting the gift, expressed the admiration and esteem in which "H.J." as he was known to his friends, had been held. It had been agreed that this trophy to be known as the "Craig Quaich" should be competed for annually along with "The Bell" and retained for a year by the skip of the winning rink. The President then presented "The Bell" and the "Craig Quaich" to David Robinson, whose rink won the Competition (13 shots up) and were the first winners of the "Craig Quaich".

Office-Bearers

Hon. President: Col. J. R. H. Hutchison, D.S.O., M.P. to 1958; John A. Warren 1959. The A.G.M. in September 1952 elected H. J. Craig, T. C. Alexander, John A. Warren, Wilson Robinson and T. K. Ward to be Life Members of the Club.

	1950–51	1951–52	1952–53	1953–54	1954–55
President:	T. G. Robinson	J. Cousland	J. Cousland	D. Carnegie	D. Carnegie
Vice-Pres.:	J. Cousland	J. A. Lyle	D. Carnegie	J. K. Craig	J. K. Craig
Rep. Members:	J. D. Cran	J. D. Cran	J. D. Cran	J. D. Cran	J. D. Cran
	A. D. Hislop	A. D. Hislop	A. D. Hislop	A. D. Hislop	D. W. Robinson

	1955–56	1956–57	1957–58	1958–59	1959–60
President:	J. K. Craig	J. A. Lyle	R. S. Pattison	E. M. Kerr	E. M. Kerr
Vice Pres.:	J. A. Lyle	R. S. Pattison	E. M. Kerr	J. A. R. Moffatt	A. Robertson

Hon. Treas.:	1950–60	D. M. McFarlane		
Hon. Sec.:	1950–58	D. W. Robinson	1958–60	E. S. McNaught
Chaplain:	1950–58	Rev. J. H. Hamilton	1958–60	Rev. A. D. Black
Ice Master:	1950–53	Geo. C. Graham	1953–59	E. M. Kerr
	1959–60	L. MacKinnon		

Committee—Members for three years—T. C. Alexander, D. Carnegie, J. K. Craig, H. J. Craig, G. R. Roxburgh, W. F. Roxburgh, R. A. French, J. Methven, E. M. Kerr, D. M. Doig, John Duncan, R. A. Smellie, J. Oswald, A. Robertson, L. MacKinnon, A Lindsay, E. S. McNaught, J. G. Robinson, E. J. Nicol, W. M. Lyle, F. C. Stewart, G. Kidd, F. E. Saunders, J. A. Carpenter, J. A. R. Moffatt, J. M. Steven.

Skips—H. J. Craig, Wilson Robinson, I. D. Scott, T. C. Alexander, J. Cousland, D. M. McFarlane, J. A. Lyle, A. D. Hislop, J. D. Cran, T. G. Robinson, D. W. Robinson, J. K. Craig, W. F. Roxburgh, D. Carnegie, John Oswald, J. A. R. Moffatt, R. S. Pattison, J. M. Steven, E. M. Kerr.

Life Members—1952: David F. Bennie and H. D. Campbell
1959: J. Kirke Craig on leaving Glasgow.

Amongst those who curled with the Club during this period were:

R. A. Smellie	A. M. O. Robertson	Alex Lindsay
J. Kirke Craig	Wilson Robinson	E. J. Jopp
W. F. Martin	J. K. Hood	R. N. Reid
J. G. Robinson	J. A. Lyle	J. R. McCrae
A. D. Hislop	J. T. R. Ward	A. D. Smith
W. F. Roxburgh	D. M. Cameron	E. S. McNaught
T. G. Robinson	W. R. Duckett	A. Frood

P. J. McVoy
Dan Macfarlane
A Bruce Maclean
T. S. Weston
J. Kirkhope
David R. Edwards
R. A. French
D. W. Robinson
G. R. Roxburgh
G. Kydd
J. M. Steven
R. S. Pattison
J. A. R. Moffatt
J. H. Bennett
J. Duncan Cran
D. W. Clow
G. C. Graham
John Duncan
T. C. Alexander
R. H. Kidd
J. Methven
D. G. Lindsay
David Carnegie

Joseph Cousland
L. Mackinnon
W. Bowie
P. J. Taggart
W. C. Collins
J. Cameron
J. Carey
A. M. Douglas
I. M. K. Fair
G. Riach
G. M. Murray
Ernest J. Nicol
R. Graham
Marcus Robinson
G. Duncan
D. K. Stirrat
V. C. V. Cowley
J. G. Stenhouse
G. M. Stewart
A. D. McCracken
G. T. Crawford
D. D. Browning
F. E. Saunders

A. A. Hems
A. Robertson
J. M. Knox
Donald S. McVean
M. Grindlay
J. McKinlay
W. B. Speirs
R. McIntosh
W. M. Lyle
T. R. Warden
C. D. A. Bird
J. Oswald
F. C. Stewart
J. A. Taggart
J. A. Carpenter
K. McLay
I. M. McNaught
Alan R. Johnston
F. H. Cameron
G. L. Ross
Tom Russell
A. L. Ross

Amongst other senior members of the Club who died during this period were Wilson Robinson, David Bennie and Isaac Scott. All had been members for many years and had curled regularly in Club games and had in their time served the Club as President and in other ways with loyalty and understanding. The Club also lost two men who had been Ice Masters and had given their help and their time in looking after the pond at Balshagray Avenue. They were Dudley Campbell and George Graham, the latter a young man in his forties who in the pre-war years had been a distinguished cricketer and Rugby player for Glasgow Academicals.

In Memoriam
Turnbull C. Alexander and Hugh J. Craig

In the Royal Club Annual 1953–54 is the following notice: "It is fitting that a joint tribute should be paid to these two curlers, who were very close friends during their life-time, and who died within a short time of one another. Turnbull Alexander on 15th

January and Hugh Craig in 11th April, 1953. For over forty years they had both been members of the Partick C. C. and had taken active parts in its management. Both had been Secretary and Representation members and Turnbull Alexander was President in 1947–48, Hugh Craig in 1933–34. They were well known to curlers in the Tenth Province and at Crossmyloof and Turnbull Alexander had officiated at many curlers' courts both as "My Lord" and his officer. Young curlers will remember the friendly encouragement freely given by both men, who were always ready to help beginners with patience and the wisdom of experience. They will be missed but not forgotten as curlers in the best aspects of the game".

Wilson Robinson. At a meeting on 29th December 1953 The President D. Carnegie referred to the recent death of Wilson Robinson, who first joined the club over fifty years ago. He was a man of the highest principles and held in great esteem both by his fellow men and brother curlers. The President said they would all remember the pleasure they had derived from his company on and off the ice, and would be grateful for all he had done for the club including his Presidency during the war years 1939–1945.

David Bennie. At the A.G.M. on 20th September 1956 The President referred to the loss the club had sustained by the death of David Bennie. He had been an office-bearer for some years and President in 1946–47. All members would mourn his passing. Both he and *Dudley Campbell* had been made life members of the club in 1952. At a meeting on 16th January 1957 the President referred to the death of Dudley Campbell who for many years had been a member and skip and office-bearer of the Club.

These greatly esteemed members had been brought up by their parents and prepared for their life and work to the accepted standard of education at that time. They were known to many of the present club members as good keen curlers so it seems appropriate to send this memorial paragraph with the story entitled "A Good Curler's Funeral Sermon" told by the Rev. James Taylor, D.D. in his book *Curling* published in Edinburgh 1884.

"The late Rev. Dr. Aiton of Dolphinton, an eccentric and humorous clergyman of the old school, had occasion to preach a funeral sermon on one of his elders, a keen curler like himself. In performing this duty after enumerating how the deceased member of session among other accomplishments could 'draw a shot' on the ice or 'strike a winner', etc. he concluded his eulogium in the following words: 'But now, my friends, he is O'er the hog-score, he's within the inner circle of eternity, and dead-guarded'."

During the decade the Club was well represented, when three rinks from the Dunbartonshire Province played against the American Curlers on 14th January 1952, and again when they played the Canadian Curlers on 20th January 1960. The only other notable Province Match during this time was the Grantown-on-Spey C.C. Centenary Bonspiel on 10th February 1956 when again Partick was represented in the Province Rink, which the author had the privilege of skipping.

The Club also continued to give very active support to all the Province Competitions, and entered rinks each year for the Kirkwood Cup, Claud Allan Cup, Claud Allan Medal, and Cuthbert Cup. Many keen and interesting games were played, although from the Partick point of view the results were generally disappointing. The other Competitions which the Club entered during this period were Royal Caledonian Curling Club Rink Championship, District Medal and the Waldie Griffith Inter-Province Cup.

Old Partick Bell Competitions

6th April 1951—At Crossmyloof, ten rinks took part, won by No. 3. J. Kirke Craig (skip) 12 shots up with A. B. McLean, A. M. O. Robertson and R. A. Smellie. Dinner after in Ice Club Restaurant with toasts and speeches—a very pleasant evening.

4th April 1952—At Crossmyloof, a record number of fourteen rinks engaged—Won by No. 5 (J. K. Craig, skip) 10 shots up with L. McKinnon, W. Bowie and Horace Bennett. After the Competition a very successful dinner was held in Downhill House, Byres Road, when the Bell and prizes were presented. Wilson Robinson and T. C. Alexander joined the dinner party which included 51 members. Speeches were made by the President (Joe Cousland), Kirke Craig, George Graham, Tom Robinson, David Carnegie, A. D. Hislop and the Hon. Secretary.

13th March 1953—At Crossmyloof Twelve rinks entered, won by No. 1 (E. M. Kerr skip)—13 shots up with D. W. Clow, E. J. Nicol, Rev. J. H. Hamilton (Chaplain). Dinner after in Downhill House, when the Honorary President Col. J. R. H. Hutchison, M.P. handed over the "Bell" and President's Prizes to the winners. The President, Joe Cousland, presided over a pleasant and convivial evening.

2nd April 1954—Twelve rinks took part at Crossmyloof— Winners No. 1 rink, 13 shots up—D. W. Robinson (skip) with G. H. Murray, Marcus Robinson and N. Foulds Martin. At the dinner after in Dowanhill House Robin Reid presented the Craig Quaich to the Club (see introductory note to this decade) and J. D. Cran, President of Dunbartonshire Province presented the "Claud Allan" Cup to Horace Bennett, Glasgow Academicals, whose rink had won it the previous evening by 7 shots from Partick. It was a pleasant evening with speeches from David Robinson, Joe Cousland, Rev. J. Hay Hamilton (Chaplain), A. D. Hislop, Marcus Robinson, George Murray and Horace Bennett.

1st April 1955—Twelve rinks took part of which No. 10 with D. W. Robinson (skip), J. Oswald, J. Carey and A. Robertson won— 13 shots up. At the dinner after in Dowanhill House The President Presented the "Bell" and Craig Quaich to the winners; and the Hon. Secretary of the "Tenth" Province presented the Claud Allan Medal to J. D. Cran as skip of the winning rink in that Competition. The R.C.C.C. Centenary Plaque was also on the table. A most successful evening followed.

29th March 1956—At Crossmyloof—Ten rinks took part, won by J. K. Craig (The President) with R. McIntosh, R. N. Reid and W. Lyle 14 shots up. Joe Cousland joined the party for dinner and an enjoyable evening was had by all.

28th March 1957—Twelve rinks took part. Rink No. 8 won, J. D. Cran (skip) with E. S. McNaught, D. M. Doig and R. C. McIntosh—13 shots up. Dinner after in Dowanhill House when the President presented the Bell and Craig Quaich and his prizes to the winning rink, and the evening was enjoyed with the usual gusto and tradition.

23rd March 1958—Twelve rinks took part, won by Rink No. 7 J. A. R. Moffatt (skip) with R. N. Reid, A. M. Douglas and T. S. Weston—13 shots up. Dinner in Dowanhill House, R. S. Pattison President in the Chair, who presented "The Bell", Craig Quaich and his prizes to the winners. Speeches were made by winners and losers. The Treasurer and Secretary and anyone else who could get a word in.

20th March 1959—Winners Rink No. 6 (J. Oswald skip) with G. T. Crawford, D. Browning and J. H. Bennett—13 shots up. Dinner after in Dowanhill House the President E. M. Kerr in the

Chair. On this occasion the club was honoured with the presence of the Chaplain, Rev. D. A. Black. The evening ended with the singing of "Auld Lang Syne" and brought another very pleasant Curling Season to a close.

17th December 1959—Partick Bell Centenary Competition. Twelve rinks engaged at Crossmyloof—Won by Rink skipped by D. W. Robinson with John Wingate, E. J. Nicol, and E. M. Kerr— 16 shots up. Centenary dinner followed (being 100 years since the Bell was first competed for by the Club). E. M. Kerr, President in the Chair presented the Bell, Craig Quaich and his prizes to the winning rink; and a Special Prize donated by the Hon. President John A. Warren to the skip of the winning rink. He expressed regret that John A. Warren, who is in his 100th year was unable to be present. A Menu Card with signatures is attached to the Minute.

Speeches at the Dinner:

The Royal Caledonian Curling Club	D. W. Robinson
Reply	Brig. J. W. H. Gow, C.B.E., D.L., J.P., President R.C.C.C.
The Partick Curling Club	John Wingate, President Tenth Dunbartonshire Province
Reply	E. M. Kerr
Old Partick Bell	J. Cousland
The Chairman	A. Robertson, Vice-President

A "Partick Bell" Day

The Annual Competitions for this Trophy probably are the most looked-forward-to and sociable events on the Partick Curling Club Calendar. All playing members want to take part in them and even the elderly youngsters enter, conveniently forgetting that, on being "made" curlers thirty or forty or more years ago they undertook "not to be a hog". If, as sweepers these old boys may be weak, the younger members in their rinks willingly compensate by putting more keen enjoyment into their efforts. The draw for rinks and their opponents has previously taken place and is a lucky-dip affair carried out by the Committee. Each rink appoints its skip on the ice. The winning rink is the one with the highest score up in shots. All through these preliminaries it is a happy-go-lucky game and in this decade winning rinks had margins of about 12 shots up more or less against their opponents. The result is that a mixture of much luck, banter and fun prevails.

It is a competition during which—In the absence of an official club umpire or even a self-appointed referee—the rules of the R.C.C.C. are not strictly observed. For example—a couple of players from a rink will take leave off the ice, for one pretext or another, because they wish to or have to, and do so without permission from their skips. The skips tend to turn a blind eye on that and other misdemeanors because they know the only reply to any remonstrance will be a wink or a glad eye!—though that may be frowned upon, if the delinquent is not at the hack when his time comes.

But the game goes on—till the time gong goes and the results are collected by the Hon. Secretary. Then the players transport themselves to Byres Road, Partick. There a number cannot resist a "short one" after their strenuous curling session in that old time houff, The Curlers Tavern, adjoining ground on which the club had a pond in early years. Thereafter, feeling more hungry than thirsty, all cross over the road for their beef and greens in Dowanhill House, which also stands on ground at one time curled on by the Partick curlers. Confirmation of this was given on 22nd May 1956 in the *Glasgow Herald*, which stated that John A. Warren, at that time Honorary President of the Club, "remembers curling in the 1870's on a marsh on the west side of Byres Road within a hundred yards of 'The Curlers'. Much earlier than this, he tells us, there was a curling on marshy ground at the point where Great George Street now joins Byres Road".

The Annual Club Dinner takes place with the President in the Chair. He presents the "Bell" and prizes to the winning rink, and asks their skip how his rink did it. This calls for speeches from winners and losers, and from any others who can get a word in or have a story to tell. Closing toasts and Auld Lang Syne end another curling season and members disperse with hopes of the next Bell Competition as a sociable event on the Club Calendar.

Record of a Curlers Court

held in the Police Gymnasium, Partick, Friday 9th February 1951. "My Lord" Wm. Filshie, Principal Asst. R. S. F. Harris. Asst. Officers—Hugh Begg, G. S. Gray.

Made Curlers	Initiates
W. Farquhar Roxburgh	E. M. Kerr
David W. Robinson	C. J. Biggart (Glasgow Accies.)
D. M. McFarlane	D. W. Clow
J. Gordon Robinson	G. R. Roxburgh
Geo. Graham	Jas. T. R. Ward
J. Kirkhope	P. J. McVoy
Jas. M. Steven	J. K. Hood
J. Kirke Craig	W. C. Collins (Bearsden)
D. R. Edward	John G. Stenhouse
W. B. Millar	T. S. Weston
R. A. Smellie	J. R. McCrae
Thos. G. Robinson	David G. Lindsay
J. Duncan Cran	A. Bruce McLean
	Alex Lindsay
	Jas. H. Smith ⎫ Glasgow
	Alistair M. Nicol ⎭ Accies.

Record of a Curlers Court

held in the Police Gymnasium, Partick, Friday 29th January 1954 whereat the following attended—"My Lord" R. S. F. Harris—His Officers, A. G. Gilmour, P. J. McLay, Arthur Frame, and the following curlers:

Made Curlers	Curlers for the making
Robin Roxburgh	Donald S. McVean
J. K. Hood	George Murray
J. R. McCrae	Frank E. Saunders
David Robinson	Ian Fair
D. M. McFarlane	Pat Taggart
J. Gordon Robinson	Lachlan McKinnon
J. Kirke Craig	John McKinlay
A. Bruce McLean	D. Browning
T. Stanley Weston	Fred Hems
Eddie Kerr	Robert Graham

Made Curlers	Curlers for the making
J. Duncan Cran	Robbie Begg
Jas. M. Steven	Archie Moffatt
Robert A. Smellie	Alex Smith
Joseph Cousland	Eric McNaught
	A. Frood
	John Oswald
	John Short
	George Riach
	Geo. G. Whyte
	Ernie Jopp
	Alex Hay
	Alex M. Douglas
	David M. Doig

1960-1970

This, the last decade of our story begins with the session 1960–61 and ends with session October 1969–March 1970. Changes took place in the management of Crossmyloof Ice Rink Co. and in the actual running of curling at the Rink. The allocation of ice to the clubs was not giving satisfaction, the ice was too often not fit to play on, and on occasion players refused to pay the increased charges, which rising costs forced the company to demand. But the number of clubs continued to increase, as did their members, and the demands for ice. So allocations to the clubs always remained on short supply. The membership of the Partick Club remained steady about 55 to 60, though for a time, owing to the poor allocation of ice a waiting list of applicants was in operation, giving priority to those with a Partick connection.

The Club subscription (annual) in 1960 was thirty shillings; in 1963 raised to £2 which included entrance fee for the recently formed league competition; and in 1966 remained at £2 for members over 25 years of age, reduced to £1 for members under 25.

It will be seen, especially to the older members, to have been a period of many major changes, some of which considerably disturbed the ground immediately surrounding the club house and rinks. The entrance gate to the ground leased from the Corporation was on the west side of Balshagray Avenue, and is now at the corner formed by the newly raised approach road to the Clyde Tunnel from Jordanhill and the North and by Victoria Park Drive North. This raised approach, with its clover-leaf earthworks and branches east and west to Dumbarton Road at varying levels entirely altered the configuration of the East end of Victoria Park and Balshagray Avenue, and unfortunately deprived the unique Curling Club House and attractive rinks of their amenity and privacy, which they had enjoyed since the first lease was granted by the Partick Burgh Corporation in 1894.

Some brief notes from the minutes are of interest, as there is often something cropping up to please, or it may be to disturb, the office-bearers and members. At the Annual General Meeting in September 1960 the Hon. Secretary pointed out that the lease for the ground would expire at Whitsunday next so the following were appointed to negotiate the best terms for a renewal with the Corporation—A. Robertson, President; D. M. McFarlane, Hon. Treasurer and E. S. McNaught, Hon. Secretary. On 8th May following the Secretary intimated that the Corporation had agreed to extend the lease for a period of seven years. P. S. McCallum was thanked for the length of rope, which he had kindly gifted to the club for fenders at the rink ends. At the A.G.M. September 1962 the Secretary stated curling had taken place at the club rink between Xmas and New Year, but with a poor attendance of members. The Representative Member, Duncan Cran, reported on the Royal Club meeting in July—that a change in the rules designed to limit the length of "slide" when delivering a stone. The new rule placed the hack or crampet further back, and limited the distance one could slide before releasing the stone. At the A.G.M. in September 1963 the Ice-Master reported that last winter there had been good ice on the pond for several weeks, though poorly attended. The new lights were a great success, thanks to the assistance of Alex Robertson. The Representative Member, D. W. Robinson reported on the R.C. Representatives' meeting—the cost of running the R.C.C.C. was, like everything these days, steadily increasing, and if it was properly to carry out its more extensive functions, it required more income. This meant substantially raising the Club's subscriptions to the Parent Body.

At a Committee Meeting in March 1964 Ice-Master L. McKinnon reported a serious leak from the club pond and was asked to get estimates for the repair. During these years, while digging and bull-dozing and earth moving continued to raise mounds and form slopes he approached the Corporation Departments and the contractors, who listened but admitted no claim for compensation by these disturbances to our property. He also approached other contractors for estimates to repair the rink. These were in the region of £200 to £300, which the club could not afford. As an alternative he then received an offer for a temporary minor repair, which was carried out in 1966; but without guarantee, though it was hoped it would be successful for a few years. During these years of disturbance the Ice-master was indefatigable in keeping an interested eye on all that was going on in the environs of the club property and he acknowledges the help he received from David Clark, Park Superintendent, in clearing obstructions from the Club House and ground.

At the A.G.M. September 1964—The Secretary stated that "applications for ice at Crossmyloof are still insufficient". The

Representative Members David Robinson and Robin Roxburgh reported that along with Duncan Cran, Representative Member for the Perth Province, they had attended the R. C. A.G.M. at Falkirk Ice Rink in July, when His Royal Highness, The Duke of Edinburgh was elected President, and thereafter other business of a formal nature was carried through.

At the A.G.M. in September 1966 the President congratulated D. W. Robinson on his appointment to the Council of the Royal Club and on the further honour he had brought to the Club. In reply David reported he had attended the meeting of the Royal Club in July, when there had been further small changes made in the rules governing "sliding" when delivering the "stones". At a committee meeting in 1966 the Treasurer reported an increased Assessment on the leased ground. This was submitted to our member, Tom Russell, who later informed the Committee that he had negotiated a reduction on the new Assessment though higher than the previous figure. In September 1967 the Secretary produced a copy print of an etching, dated 1930 by Duncan Cran of the Victoria Park Gates in Balshagray Avenue at that time. The gates, now removed to Victoria Park Drive North, had been presented by the ladies of Partick for the formal opening of the Park in June 1887, when the Captain of the Guard of Honour on that occasion was the late Wilson Robinson, a past President of the Partick C.C. At the A.G.M. in September 1968 the Representative Member J. M. Steven reported on attending the Royal Club A.G.M. at Peebles in July when there was discussion on penalties being imposed (for a trial period of a year) for late attendance at matches. This caused some concern, as perhaps not being in the spirit of curling. It appeared that all the ladies' clubs were very well represented, and this made an impression on our batchelor representative.

For some time a "Club-tie" had been under discussion and A. D. Smith and N. S. Wilson were requested to put their heads together for their considered opinion. This they successfully did, the sample they submitted met with unanimous approval, and it has found favour and been worn by the members. Earlier in the year the Secretary reported the lease for the ground at Victoria Park had expired. The Town Clerk and the Director of Parks were agreeable to renewal, so the President with the Treasurer and the Secretary were authorised to sign a new lease for further seven years. The A.G.M. in September recorded a hearty vote of thanks to

R. M. Davidson for his great assistance to the Secretary by having the Club circulars to members prepared for distribution. At the A.G.M. on 2nd October 1969 the Ice-master reported a meeting had been arranged for the 4th inst. with a Representative of Messrs. Balfour Beatty to discuss what reparation they were prepared to make for the damage sustained by the Pond, whilst the Tunnel Road Works were being carried out. He was hopeful that a suitable recompense would be forthcoming. At a Committee Meeting in February 1970 this matter was still unsettled. On 2nd March the President informed the Committee that Frank H. Cameron had agreed to undertake the office of Honorary Secretary, and the meeting expressed their gratitude to Frank.

At the Dunbartonshire Province A.G.M. on 20th November 1969 D. W. Robinson was elected President of the Province

Office-Bearers

Hon. President John A. Warden, A. D. Hislop, J. Cousland and J. D. Cran.

	1960–61	1961–62	1962–63	1963–64	1964–65
President:	A. Robertson	L. Mackinnon	G. Kidd	D. W. Robinson	J. Duncan
Vice-Pres.:	L. Mackinnon	G. Kidd	D. W. Robinson	J. Duncan	David Doig
Rep. Members:	D. W. Robinson	D. W. Robinson	D. W. Robinson	D. W. Robinson	D. W. Robinson
	D. Carnegie	J. D. Cran	J. D. Cran	G. R. Roxburgh	G. R. Roxburgh

	1965–66	1966–67	1967–68
President:	D. M. Doig	J. M. Steven	A. D. Smith
Vice President:	J. M. Steven	A. Smith	T. R. Warden
Rep. Members:	D. W. Robinson	D. W. Robinson	D. W. Robinson
	G. R. Roxburgh	J. M. Steven	J. M. Steven

	1968–69	1696–70	1970–71
President:	T. R. Warden	E. S. McNaught	W. Bowie
Vice- President:	E. S. McNaught	Wm. Bowie	G. R. Roxburgh
Rep. Members:	D. W. Robinson	D. W. Robinson	D. W. Robinson
	J. M. Steven	J. M. Steven	J. M. Steven

Hon. Treas.:	1960–71	D. M. McFarlane
Hon. Sec.:	1960–66	E. S. McNaught
	1966–68	L. Mackinnon
	1968–70	W. D. A. Taggart
	1970–71	F. H. Cameron
Chaplain:	1960–62	Rev. David Herd, M.A.
	1962–71	Rev. Keith McRobb
Ice Master:	1962–71	L. Mackinnon

Committee—F. C. Stewart, W. M. Lyle, F. E. Saunders, G. Kidd, J. A. Carpenter, J. Oswald, G. R. Roxburgh, W. Bowie, A. Robertson, F. H. Cameron, T. Russell, J. M. Steven, T. R. Warden, Alex

Smith, N. S. Wilson, E. M. Kerr, D. K. Stirrat, R. M. Davidson, J. G. Robinson, M. C. Kirkwood, D. H. Hall, J. K. Hood, R. N. Reid, J. Ross.

Skips—J. D. Cran, D. W. Robinson, E. M. Kerr, D. Carnegie, T. G. Robinson, D. M. McFarlane, G. Kidd, J. Oswald, A. Robertson, T. Russell, R. N. Reid, W. B. Speirs, J. Duncan, D. M. Doig, W. Bowie, J. M. Steven, W. M. Lyle, Alex Smith, G. R. Roxburgh, T. R. Warden, F. H. Cameron, G. Murray.

Life Members—J. S. Cousland, J. A. Lyle, J. K. Craig.

Among those who curled with the Club during this period were:

D. Clark	A. B. McLean	R. M. Davidson
J. Carey	J. D. Cran	R. Bissett
R. N. Reid	I. M. McNaught	J. A. Steven
D. M. Doig	J. A. R. Moffatt	W. D. A. Taggart
A. R. Johnston	E. M. Kerr	W. Ferguson
E. S. McNaught	D. M. McFarlane	P. W. Richmond
W. M. Lyle	A. Frood	M. W. Muir
T. R. Warden	F. H. Cameron	J. M. Wilson
J. K. Hood	J. A. Taggart	A. Aitken
G. R. Roxburgh	L. Mackinnon	D. H. Hall
M. Robinson	A. Robertson	M. C. Kirkwood
J. M. Steven	G. Crawford	D. G. McCrae
D. W. Robinson	W. C. McClure	K. Walker
J. Oswald	A. Lindsay	G. M. M. Drum-
J. H. Bennett	W. C. Collins	mond
A. D. Smith	R. C. McIntosh	T. Anderson
P. J. McVoy	A. M. Douglas	J. H. Latta
J. A. Carpenter	T. S. Weston	J. Tennant
F. E. Saunders	W. Bowie	T. Russell
J. G. Robinson	J. D. Fraser	V. G. Weston
E. A. Brockett	N. S. Wilson	R. Day
P. J. Taggart	A. L. Ross	J. B. McCreath
C. D. A. Bird	J. Ross	R. G. Graham
J. K. Craig	R. Robinson	N. S. Mathieson
A. D. Hislop	W. B. Speirs	P. E. McSween
G. H. Murray	B. Wilson	H. T. Shirley
J. Duncan	A. Fowler	D. Walker
J. Wingate	D. D. Browning	E. Southward
G. Kidd	D. Findlay	T. L. K. Graham
I. M. K. Fair	J. O. Lennox	J. T. Munro
D. K. Stirrat		W. Stewart

The death of John A. Warren on 28th March, 1961, in his 101st year was the last personal connection the Club had with the nineteenth century. He was actively concerned with the construction of the present Club Rink in Victoria Park in 1894 and could recall curling taking place in ponds near Byres Road in the early 1880's. He was Club President in 1932.

It is fitting to recall the deaths during the 1960's of three other Past Presidents, Alex D. Hislop who died within a few days of his ninetieth birthday and up to a fortnight previously had been curling regularly; James A. Lyle and Joe Cousland. All three in their own way had given long and loyal service to the Club over many years.

Partick Curling Club has played regularly in the Province and in other curling competitions but it would be wearisome to go into these in detail. The most successful year was in 1966–67 when the Kirkwood Cup, the R.C.C.C. Province Medal and the Cuthbert Cup were won. Friendly matches were played against Glasgow Academicals, Twenty Club, Watsonians, Clydesdale Bank, Bearsden, Bank of Scotland and Glasgow Conservative Clubs. Matches for a R.C.C.C. District medal took place bienially and victories were recorded against Dumbarton and Glasgow Twenty Club and losses incurred against Barr, Galston Haymouth and Pollok.

During this decade touring teams visited Scotland and played against the Tenth Province. These included Canadians, Americans, Norwegians, Swiss, French and Swedish curlers. The following members of Partick played in one or more of these matches; Horace Bennett, Duncan Cran, Dan McFarlane, Gordon Robinson, John Oswald, John Wingate and David Robinson.

David Robinson also had the honour of captaining the first R.C.C.C. team to visit Switzerland in January 1967 and curled on several occasions for the Royal Club in the annual match against England, played alternately in Edinburgh and London. He was senior Vice-President of the R.C.C.C. in 1970–71.

That these contests have been and are played in enjoyable carefree conditions goes without saying, while the same happy go lucky atmosphere prevails. This is as we desire and as it should be, because we are friendly clubs in a classless society, and are reminded of the story told by the Rev. James Taylor, D.D. of Dolphinton, Lanarkshire, in the Preface to his *Curling*, Published Edinburgh, 1884—as—

"an example of Audacious wit"

"The late Sheriff Burnett of Peebles (1865–66) a worthy man and keen curler, was playing with J.H. a well-known Peebles character, a stone mason by trade, a first class curler, but a noted river poacher. Indeed, the Sheriff had, nearly every winter to send him to prison for illegal fishing. On the present occasion the poacher was skip, and the Sheriff was about to play, when the former addressed him thus: "I say Shirra, dae ye see that stane?" "Aye Jock," answered the Sheriff. "A' weel, Shirra" says Jock, pointing to the stone with his kowe—"just gie that ane sixty days".

The "Partick Bell" Days

As described in an earlier page, these are the most sociable in the Club Calendar, beginning late afternoon at Crossmyloof with the "Bell" Competition, followed by the Annual Dinner in Dowanhill House.

On 24th March 1961—Ten rinks had entered, and the rink skipped by F. E. Saunders with P. J. McVoy, J. A. Carpenter and A. D. Smith won with 9 shots up. President A. Robertson, The Rev. David Herd "present with us for the first time". He then presented "The Bell' and prizes to the winners. Speeches and stories followed till "Auld Lang Syne" finished the evening about 10.10 p.m.

On 30th March 1962—The skip of the winning rink W. C. Collins with D. M. Doig, F. H. Cameron and D. A. Bird was presented by the President L. McKinnon with the prizes, the winning skip with the Craig Quaich, and the "Bell" as no member of the rink resided in Partick, was taken into custody by the President, who presided at the Annual Dinner.

22nd March 1963—Won by rink skipped by J. D. Cran, with J. A. Carpenter, R. N. Reid and R. C. McIntosh. The Annual Dinner thereafter was held in the Hamilton Crescent Hotel, Glasgow, W.4, where our new Chaplain and Guest, Rev. Keith McRobb was introduced by President Gordon Kidd, who then handed prizes to the winning rink. This was followed by speeches from J. D. Cran and T. G. Robinson and other members of the company. Following the speeches a very interesting film, taken at the Grand March at Lake of Menteith was shown by Alex Smith. A most enjoyable evening concluded by singing "Auld Lang Syne".

24th March, 1964—Ten rinks took part in the competition which was won by rink skipped by D. M. McFarlane with P. J. McVoy,

A. Lindsay and R. Robinson. As the skip lived outwith the pre-
scribed boundary P. J. McVoy became custodian of "The Bell".
The Annual Dinner followed in Dowanhill House. The President
David Robinson in the chair, supported by the Chaplain, Rev.
Keith McRobb. The Hon. President A. D. Hislop who skipped a
rink in the afternoon "Bell" Competition and who celebrated his
eighty-eighth birthday a few weeks ago, J. K. Craig and J. Cousland,
Life Members. After Dinner, prior to giving out the prizes the
President gave a most interesting account of the known history of the
"Bell" which dates back to 1726. This was followed by speeches and
stories from various members including J. Cousland and the Padre
till 10.45 when the President drew a most successful evening to a
close.

1st April 1965—Ten rinks competed, won by rink four skipped by
T. G. Robinson, 11 shots up, with P. J. Taggart, R. N. Reid and
G. H. Murray. As no member of the winning rink resided within
the prescribed boundary, it was agreed that the losing skip J. K.
Hood would "keep" the "Bell" for the ensuing twelve months.
The Annual Dinner followed in Dowanhill House, the President
John Duncan in the Chair. He regretted that our Hon. President
Alex Hislop, who recently celebrated his eighty-ninth birthday, was
unable to be present. He then presented prizes to the winning
rink, to T. G. Robinson the Craig Quaich and to J. K. Hood the
"Bell".

After the usual speeches and stories the evening concluded with
"Auld Lang Syne" at 10.45.

29th March 1966—Eight rinks competed. Rink No. 8 skipped
by John Oswald won (10 shots up) with R. N. Reid, G. Kidd and
D. K. Stirrat. The Annual Dinner after was presided over by
David Doig, President. He referred to the loss to the club of two
of its oldest members who recently passed away. The Hon. President A. D. Hislop, who died a few days before his ninetieth birthday
day and J. A. Lyle who had been in poor health for some years.
The President then handed over the competition prizes to the
winning rink—the Craig Quaich to John Oswald and the "Bell" as
no member of his rink resided within the prescribed boundary to
the Vice-President Jim Steven for safe keeping. Speeches and
stories and "Auld Lang Syne" at 10.30 brought a happy evening
to a close.

19th March 1967—Ten rinks competed. No. 8 skipped by T. S.

Weston (16 shots up) won with L. McKinnon, R. Bisset, and I. M.
McNaught. The Annual Dinner in Dowanhill House was presided
over by J. M. Steven, President, in the Chair. It was a happy one
for the President, who had on the table two Province Trophies won
by the Club, the Kirkwood Cup and the Cuthbert Cup. On the
President's invitation all members present partook of Drambuie
Liqueur from one of the cups, with coffee. Jim Steven mentioned
that Partick reached another final, and, due to an unfortunate
misunderstanding, did not have a chance to play-off. The Club
also received two Royal Club Medals—one which goes to the winners of the Kirkwood Cup and a District Medal for winning a R.C.
District Match.

27th March 1968—Ten rinks competed. The winning rink was
skipped by E. M. Kerr (11 shots) with D. H. Hall, J. A. R. Moffatt
and E. S. McNaught. The Annual Dinner, with the largest attendance for some years, was presided over by President A. D. Smith
and the evening most successful. The President's hospitality by
way of Drambuies was most acceptable, although there was no
Province Cup on display! The President presented the prizes to the
winners and to the skip, who resides within the Burgh, who holds
both the "Bell" and the Quaich. He also presented the skip, John
Oswald, of the winning League Rink, with the League Trophy.
The President then called on several members to speak. The Rev.
Keith McRobb, Archie Moffatt from Edinburgh, Kirke Craig who
ventured down from Oban to join the fun. Before "Auld Lang
Syne" T. R. Warden, Vice-President (in dinner-jacket before
proceeding to another and lesser function), proposed a vote of thanks
to the President, who was acclaimed a very happy evening.

28th March 1969—Ten rinks competing, of which rink No. 9
skipped by D. M. McFarlane (12 shots up) won with A. Moffatt,
L. McKinnon and O. Lennox. The Annual Dinner in Dowanhill
House with President T. R. Warden in the chair. He remarked on
the lower than usual attendance owing to a "flu" epidemic. He
entrusted custody of the "Bell" to L. McKinnon, as the skip
D. McFarlane lived outside the prescribed boundary and was
presented with the Craig Quaich. He also presented prizes to the
winning rink, and the League Trophy to W. Bowie, whose rink vied
with that of J. M. Steven on games won, but won the aggregate of
shots up. After presenting the prizes the President called on several
members to speak, including Duncan Cran who gave a most

interesting resume of his researches into the history of the club, and Kirke Craig, D. W. Robinson and Lachie McKinnon. The President was enthusiastically thanked for a successful evening, which ended with "Auld Lang Syne".

PARTICK CURLING CLUB
Winning Skips of the Old Partick Bell Competition

Year	Skip	Year	Skip
1859	John White	1938	T. D. Carpenter
1860	John Dunn	1939	A. D. Hislop
1871	Archibald Anderson	1940–46	No Competition
1875	John Anderson	1947	W. Foulds Martin
1880	John Anderson	1948	J. Duncan Cran
1885	Archibald Anderson	1949	A. D. Hislop
1886	Archibald Anderson	1950	W. Foulds Martin
1895	John Anderson	1951	J. Kirke Craig
1897	W. Sutherland	1952	J. Kirke Craig
1899	M. H. Kennedy	1953	E. M. Kerr
1901	R. Lindsay	1954	D. W. Robinson
1902	William McColl	1955	D. W. Robinson
1903	James T. Ward	1956	J. Kirke Craig
1911	J. G. Kennedy	1957	J. Duncan Cran
1912	W. Ward	1958	J. A. R. Moffatt
1913	J. G. Kennedy	1959	John Oswald
1914	M. H. Kennedy	1959	(December) Centenary Competition
1915	J. G. Kennedy		D. W. Robinson
1916	D. Muirhead	1961	F. E. Saunders
1917	W. L. Duncan	1962	W. C. Collins
1918	W. L. Duncan	1963	J. D. Cran
1922	M. Hunter Kennedy	1964	D. M. MacFarlane
1925	M. Hunter Kennedy	1965	T. G. Robinson
1929	John A. Warren	1966	John Oswald
1933	Rev. J. Mitchell Kerr	1967	T. Stanley Weston
1934	Robert Craig	1968	E. M. Kerr
1935	Isaac D. Scott	1969	D. M. McFarlane
1936	R. Allan Ogg	1970	D. M. Doig
1937	James Jackson		

Record of a Curlers' Court

Held in Glasgow Academical Clubhouse on Friday 21st January 1968, whereat the following attended—"My Lord" A. M. Frame. His Officers—and the following Curlers.

Made Curlers	Curlers for the Making	
David W. Robinson	David Clark	D. K. Stirratt
Alistair M. Nicol	T. Ogilvie Lennox	Tom Anderson
J. K. Hood	R. C. McIntosh	D. J. McCrae
A. D. Smith	M. W. Muir	R. M. Davidson
L. McKinnon	N. S. Wilson	W. C. McClure
D. M. Doig	J. A. Taggart	M. C. Kirkwood
John Inglis	I. M. McNaught	D. H. Hall
G. R. Roxburgh	A. Aitken	
John Duncan		
D. M. McFarlane		
E. S. McNaught		
Ian Fair		
F. Russell		
J. Duncan Cran		

The proceeds of the stoup amounted to £10 10 0 and were distributed on the unanimous vote of the Members as follows:

£5 5 0 to the R.C.C.C. Building Fund

£5 5 0 to the Scottish Schoolboys' Club.

The Treasurers of both these Funds acknowledged the gifts made by the Academical Club and the Partick Club.

Roll of Honour—1914–18
Partick Curling Club

Members loyally serving King and Country. Great War 1914–1918—illuminated with—Coat of Arms, Old Partick Bell, Union Jack and Scottish Standard and with good drawing of Club House, Partick by R. S. Anderson.

Killed in Action

G. G. Henderson	Highland Light Infantry
Archibald J. Kemp	Highland Light Infantry

Roll of Service

Turnbull C. Alexander	Highland Light Infantry
Robert J. Borthwick	Highland Light Infantry
Hugh J. Craig	Highland Light Infantry
James Craig	R.N.V.R. attached R.N.A.S.
Farquhar Gracie	R.A.M.C.
John Gracie	R.A.M.C.

William Lamont	Royal Field Artillery
Francis Rorke	Argyll and Sutherland Highlanders
H. R. Taggart	Highland Light Infantry
G. K. Walker	Army Pay Corps
A. E. Ward	R.A.M.C.
Thomas K. Ward	Argyll and Sutherland Highlanders

Roll of Honour 1939–1945
Partick Curling Club

Members loyally serving King and Country. Second World War 1939–1945 illuminated with Partick Coat of Arms, Old Partick Bell, Union Jack and Scottish Standard with drawing of Club House by T. M. Gray, 1953.

Roll of Honour

I. M. Moyes	Royal Corps of Signals
R. Allan Ogg	Highland Light Infantry
T. W. Ward	Royal Air Force

Roll of Service

J. Kirke Craig	R.N.V.S.R.
J. Methven	Royal Air Force
T. M. Niven	Royal Corps of Signals
R. S. Pattison	Royal Observer Corps
A. M. O. Robertson	Royal Artillery
D. W. Robinson	Highland Light Infantry
T. G. Robinson	Glasgow Highlanders
R. A. Smellie	Ayrshire Yeomanry

Partick Curling Club
Secretaries

1842–43	James Borthwick
1844–47	John Smellie
1848–53	James Borthwick
1854–62	Thomas Granger
1863–68	Andrew Hosie
1869–84	Arch. Anderson
1885–98	David Muirhead
1899–	G. Kirkwood
1900–10	Wm. Ward

1911–19   John Lamont
1919–23   R. A. Smellie
1924–33   H. J. Craig
1934–45   T. C. Alexander
1946–58   David W. Robinson
1958–66   E. S. McNaught
1966–68   L. MacKinnon
1968–70   W. D. A. Taggart
1970–   F. H. Cameron

List of Members 1970–1971

Joined

Hon. President
1930   J. Duncan Cran, 6 Hughenden Terrace, W.2.
        Chaplain
1963   Rev. Keith McRobb, M.A., 20 St. Kilda Dr., W.4.
        Life Member
1928   J. K. Craig, Rock Cottage, Clachan Seil, by Oban.
        Ordinary Members
1968   Allan Aitken, 38 Woodvale Avenue, Clarkston.
1967   Prof. T. Anderson, 52 Kingsborough Gds., W.2.
1951   W. Bowie, 20 Whittingehame Drive, W.2.
1953   D. D. Browning, 25 Sutherland Ave., S.1.
1937   Horace Bennett, Loudonhill Inn, Darvel.
1969   E. A. Brockett, 68 Braeside Ave., Milngavie.
1959   F. H. Cameron, 12 Garngaber Avenue, Lenzie.
1960   David Clark, 12 Victoria Park Drive North, W.2.
1965   R. M. Davidson, 33 Kingsborough Gardens, W.2.
1951   D. M. Doig, 14 Collylinn Road, Bearsden.
1948   John Duncan, 48 Blair Road, Coatbridge.
1968   Richard Day, 181 Meadowburn, Bishopbriggs.
1969   G. M. M. Drummond, 18 Whittingehame Drive, W.2.
1959   J. D. Fraser, Newfield, Bearsden.
1965   A. D. Finlay, 17 Waterside Road, Carmunnock.
1969   W. Ferguson, 6 Herries Road, S.1.
1970   R. G. Graham, 44 Kingsborough Gardens, W.2.
1970   T. L. K. Graham, 8 Beaton Road, S.1.
1967   Douglas H. Hall, 5 Kingsborough Gardens, W.2.
1950   J. K. Hood, 16 Marlborough Avenue, W.1.
1958   A. R. Johnstone, 98 Whittingehame Court, W.2.

Joined

Ordinary Members—cont.

1949 E. M. Kerr, 3 Naseby Avenue, W.1.
1956 M. Kirkwood, 50 Kingsborough Gardens, W.2.
1950 Alex Lindsay, 74 Kintore Road, S.3.
1955 W. M. Lyle, 56 Cleveden Drive, W.2.
1965 J. Ogilvie Lennox, 21 East Montrose Street, Helensburgh.
1968 J. H. Latta, 10 Sandringham Avenue, Newton Mearns.
1970 J. T. Munro, 13 Torridon Avenue, S.1.
1970 N. S. Matheson, 29 Randolph Road, W.1.
1951 G. M. Murray, Millburn Cottage, Skelmorlie.
1967 Matt. W. Muir, 29 Pendicle Road, Bearsden.
1949 J. A. R. Moffatt, 13 Seton Place, Edinburgh 9 WP.
1968 W. C. McClure, 78 Novar Drive, W.2.
1955 R. C. McIntosh, 47 Langside Drive, S.3.
1952 L. McKinnon, 6 Marlborough Avenue, W.1.
1931 D. M. McFarlane, 94 Norse Road, W.4.
1948 A. B. McLean, 19 Pentrith Avenue, Giffnock.
1949 P. J. McVoy, 46 Balshagray Avenue, W.1.
1965 D. G. Macrae, 9 Lonsdale Avenue, Giffnock.
1952 E. S. McNaught, 42 Kingsborough Gardens, W.2.
1959 I. M. McNaught, 44 Southbrae Drive, W.3.
1969 John B. McCreath, 43 St. Kilda Drive, W.4.
1951 John Oswald, Howmains, Glencaple, Dumfries.
1953 R. N. Reid, 36 Thorn Road, Bearsden.
1936 D. W. Robinson, Lyndos, Abercromby Street East, Helensburgh.
1947 J. Gordon Robinson, 40 Stirling Drive, Bearsden.
1950 Marcus Robinson, Rockfort, Craigendoran, Helensburgh.
1938 T. G. Robinson, Winder, Drumclog Avenue, Milngavie.
1963 R. Robinson, Little Dunkyan, Killearn.
1959 A. L. Ross, 5 Roselea Gardens, W.3.
1966 J. M. Ross, 5 Roselea Gardens, W.3.
1947 G. R. Roxburgh, 12A Bruce Road, S.1.
1959 Tom Russell, 36 Victoria Park Gardens South, W.1.
1969 P. W. Richmond, 92 Hyndland Road, W.2.
1970 E. Southward, 10 Herries Road, S.1.
1970 H. T. Shirley, 28 Beaconsfield Road, W.2.
1948 J. M. Steven, 9 Princes Terrace, W.2.
1966 J. A. Steven, Ardshealach, Helensburgh.

1953   A. D. Smith, 14 Stewart Drive, Clarkston.
1955   W. B. Speirs, Baldernock Glebe, Milngavie.
1958   D. K. Stirratt, 17 Monreith Road, S.3.
1952   P. J. Taggart, 3 Arnwood Drive, W.2.
1955   J. A. Taggart, Wester Hayston, Kirkintilloch.
1966   W. D. A. Taggart, 7 Woodville Road, Newport, Mon.
1967   John Tennant, 35 Victoria Crescent Road, W.2.
1948   T. Stanley Weston, Nether Shandon, Coldrush Road,
       Drymen.
1968   V. G. Weston, 20 Hamilton Drive, W.2.
1956   T. R. Warden, 3 West Chapelton Lane, Bearsden.
1960   John Wingate, 7 Collylin Road, Bearsden.
1963   N. S. Wilson, 30 Beaconsfield Road, W.2.
1968   Dr. Keith Walker, Dept. of Clinical Pathology (Bio-
       chemistry) University Hospital, Edmonton, Alberta,
       Canada.
1970   D. Walker, 134 Hyndland Road, W.2.
1970   P. E. McSween, 60 Balshagray Avenue, W.1.

Partick Curling Club
Presidents

1842–43	John McMaster	1897–99	William Kennedy
1843–45	John Anderson	1899–1902	William McColl
1845–50	William Anderson	1902–08	M. Hunter Kennedy
1850–54	John White	1910–12	James T. Ward
1854–55	Peter McGaw	1912–14	J. Guthrie Kennedy
1855–56	John Smith	1914–20	David Muirhead
1856–57	John Anderson	1920–21	Robert Robinson
1857–58	Archibald Anderson	1921–29	J. M. Lamont
1858–59	James Brownlie	1929–31	David Robinson
1859–60	Archibald Anderson	1931–33	John A. Warren
1860–61	John Dunn	1933–35	H. J. Craig
1861–62	A. Roy	1935–37	Dr. John Gracie
1862–63	A. Hosie	1937–45	Wilson Robinson
1863–64	Thomas Granger	1945–46	T. K. Ward
1864–65	Robert Barbour	1946–47	D. F. Bennie
1865–66	Thomas Smith	1947–48	T. C. Alexander
1866–67	John McGilchrist	1948–49	J. Duncan Cran
1867–68	John Phillips	1949–50	A. D. Hislop
1868–69	John Maxwell	1950–51	T. G. Robinson

1869–70	John Clark	1951–53	Joseph Cousland
1870–71	John Thomson	1953–55	D. Carnegie
1871–72	John Auchinclass	1955–56	J. Kirke Craig
1872–73	David More	1956–57	Jas. A. Lyle
1873–74	William Kirkwood	1957–58	R. S. Pattison
1874–75	D. Campbell	1958–60	E. M. Kerr
1875–76	Thomas Fletcher	1960–61	A. Robertson
1876–78	R. D. Samuels	1961–62	L. McKinnon
1878–79	John Orr	1962–63	G. Kidd
1879–80	William Frame	1963–64	D. W. Robinson
1880–81	John Stewart	1964–65	J. Duncan
1881–82	Archibald Livingston	1965–66	D. M. Doig
1882–84	John Anderson	1966–67	J. M. Steven
1884–85	Wm. Sutherland	1967–68	Alex D. Smith
1885–87	John Anderson	1968–69	T. R. Warden
1887–93	John W. Robinson	1969–70	E. S. McNaught
1893–95	James Watson	1970–71	W. Bowie
1895–97	Matthew White